From Alabama to Margraten

MIEKE KIRKELS

From Alabama to Margraten

THE STORY OF WAR VETERAN
JEFFERSON WIGGINS
IN THE SEGREGATED US ARMY
DURING WORLD WAR II

LONDON AND NEW YORK

The publication of this book is made possible by grants from
The Netherlands embassy to the United States in Washington, DC
The Netherlands America Foundation
The municipality of Eijsden-Margraten
The Kanunnik Salden Foundation
The John Adams Institute

Originally published in Dutch as:
Mieke Kirkels, *Van Alabama naar Margraten. Jefferson Wiggins' herinneringen aan zijn diensttijd in het gesegregeerde Amerikaanse bevrijdingsleger*. Uitgever Alabama, 2014, and Uitgeverij Leon van Dorp, 2023 (second edition)

First published in 2025 by Amsterdam University Press Ltd.

Published 2025 by Routledge
4 Park Square, Milton Park, Abingdon, Oxon OX14 4RN
605 Third Avenue, New York, NY 10158

Routledge is an imprint of the Taylor & Francis Group, an informa business

© M. Kirkels / Taylor & Francis Group 2025

All rights reserved. No part of this book may be reprinted or reproduced or utilised in any form or by any electronic, mechanical, or other means, now known or hereafter invented, including photocopying and recording, or in any information storage or retrieval system, without permission in writing from the publishers.

Trademark notice: Product or corporate names may be trademarks or registered trademarks, and are used only for identification and explanation without intent to infringe.

ISBN: 9789040368369 (pbk)
ISBN: 9781003696087 (ebk)

NUR   694

Cover illustration: Jefferson Wiggins, May 4, 2009, in New Fairfield, Connecticut (Photo: Albert Elings, Ruim Kader Films)

Cover design: Suzan Beijer

Translated from Dutch by Frans Kooymans

DOI   10.5117/9789048568369

Every effort has been made to obtain permission to use all copyrighted illustrations reproduced in this book. Nonetheless, whosoever believes to have rights to this material is advised to contact the publisher.

For Product Safety Concerns and Information please contact our EU representative: GPSR@taylorandfrancis.com
Taylor & Francis Verlag GmbH, Kaufingerstraße 24, 80331 München, Germany

"I've learned that people will forget what you said, people will forget what you did, but people will never forget how you made them feel."

– Maya Angelou

Table of Contents

Foreword   11

Preface   13

Preface to this Edition   15

Introduction   19

Introduction to this Edition   23

CHAPTER 1 – Houston County, Alabama   27

CHAPTER 2 – A Segregated Crossing to Scotland   51

CHAPTER 3 – Digging Graves   65

CHAPTER 4 – The Fields of Margraten   73

CHAPTER 5 – The Netherlands American Cemetery and Memorial   85

CHAPTER 6 – American Policy against Racism in Wartime   97

CHAPTER 7 – Professional Soldier or Civilian?   107

CHAPTER 8 – A Long Career in Education   123

CHAPTER 9 – Lessons of Margraten 125

CHAPTER 10 – Back to Margraten: A Telephone Call from the Past 129

CHAPTER 11 – Margraten 2009 139

CHAPTER 12 – People Should Know! 145

CHAPTER 13 – A Follow-up Oral History Project 149

CHAPTER 14 – People Should Know, the Sequel 151

Epilogue by Jonathan Pieterse 165

Acknowledgements 169

Literature 173

Jefferson Wiggins in September 2009 in Margraten, the Netherlands, after the presentation of *From Farmfield to Soldiers Cemetery* (Photo: J.P. Geussens)

Words by Jefferson Wiggins

This story is substantially based on facts. I say "substantially" because it was not written from notes or records but rather from memories. At the time of the most compelling and formative experiences of this story, I was young, uneducated and unsophisticated. I had little vision of a future for myself, much less a vision that more than fifty years into the future I would have any reason to write these words or that others would have any reason to read them. So this work is built from memories. Over the years, some memories have faded, others have crystallized, and still others have been shaped by the perspective of time, experience and emotion.

> The story is as I remember it, as I remember experiencing it. Some may remember it differently. Others may choose to forget altogether because of the pain and humiliation that is involved.

This story is written in the third person, yet it is about me. I have used the real names of characters. In writing this story, I found myself alternating between the first and third persons. Some memories were too painful to commit to paper in the first person. Yet the experiences upon which this work is based were far too personal to ascribe to characters with fictitious names. So the work stands as it is. This struggle for perspective, in itself, speaks volumes to the impact of these events and memories on my life.

Jefferson Wiggins, *Another Generation Almost Forgotten* (pag 13: Xlibris, 2003)

Foreword

Jefferson Wiggins' memories are both powerful and essential to understanding the complexities of war and the sacrifices made by so many. His story not only highlights the hardships he and his fellow African American soldiers endured, but also serves as a stark reminder of the inequalities that persisted even during a time of global conflict.

Jefferson Wiggins served as a first sergeant in the segregated 960th Quartermaster Service Company of the US Army. His unit's mission was to dig the graves and bury the soldiers who were killed in the war in the Netherlands American Cemetery in Margraten.

When Wiggins returned to Margraten, he discovered how little the Dutch knew about the racial segregation in the US Army during World War II. It was thanks to his determination that this forgotten chapter of history came to light.

Mieke Kirkels, who worked with Jefferson Wiggins to

document his memories, has made an invaluable contribution to our understanding of our shared history in the Netherlands and the United States with "From Alabama to Margraten." This book brings new insights and details to the story of the African American troops in the Netherlands, deepening our awareness of their experiences.

As the Dutch Ambassador to the United States, I am especially grateful for the efforts of Mieke Kirkels. This book is not just a tribute to Jefferson Wiggins and his fellow soldiers, but also a call to all of us to keep exploring and understanding history in all its aspects. It reminds us that the fight for freedom and equality, both then and now, often left many in the shadows. We must continue to share their stories so that their sacrifices are never forgotten.

I am also glad that this important book is now available in English, making it accessible to a worldwide audience. The story of Jefferson Wiggins and the African American troops in Margraten deserves to be told far and wide because it is a testament to the strength and heroism of those valiant men.

I hope it resonates deeply with readers everywhere.

Birgitta Tazelaar
Ambassador of the Kingdom of the Netherlands to the United States

Preface

More than one million African American men and women served in the US armed forces in World War II. Sixteen thousand of them were stationed in the Netherlands.

Their stories, presented here in Mieke Kirkels' book, *From Alabama to Margraten*, are vitally important for understanding the contributions that Black troops made to the war effort. African American soldiers were assigned to racially segregated units, largely toiling in service and supply roles.

In her earlier work, Kirkels recorded and shared the memories of Jefferson Wiggins, who arrived in the Netherlands as a nineteen-year-old first sergeant in the 960th Quartermaster Service Company of the US Army. Wiggins and his unit dug burial plots at the Netherlands American Cemetery, in the village of Margraten. The work was backbreaking and emotionally devastating.

Part of the power of these stories is that Wiggins and

other Black soldiers served proudly during the war at a time when America treated them as second-class citizens. The rallying cry for Black Americans during World War II was "Double Victory", as they fought to achieve victory both over fascism abroad and over racism at home. They understood it was not enough to defeat the Nazis and the Axis powers in Europe, only to come home to racial discrimination in the United States.

When Black veterans returned to America after the war ended, they kept fighting, with many becoming leaders in the civil rights movement. For too long the story of the vast contributions that African American troops made to the war effort have been erased from our history books. Mieke Kirkels has done pioneering work to make visible the stories of Black Liberators in the Netherlands. I hope readers learn as much from this book as I did.

Matthew F. Delmont
Sherman Fairchild Distinguished Professor of History at Dartmouth College
Author of *Half American: The Epic Story of African Americans Fighting World War II at Home and Abroad* (New York: Viking, 2022)

Preface to this Edition

The first edition of this book was published in November 2014. Jefferson Wiggins had passed away the year before, on January 9, 2013. The book led to many reactions in the Netherlands. Until then, few people in the Netherlands knew anything about the involvement of Black American soldiers in the liberation from Nazi Germany. Some years earlier, in 2009, Jefferson Wiggins already spoke of that involvement in the book *Van boerenakker tot soldatenkerkhof* (published in English as *From Farmland to Soldiers Cemetery*) and in the documentary *Akkers van Margraten* (*Fields of Margraten*).*

Jeff was invited to join the presentation of that book and the documentary in Margraten in September 2009.

---

* Mieke Kirkels, Jo Purnot, and Frans Roebroeks, *From Farmland to Soldiers Cemetery: Eye Witness Accounts of the Construction of the American Cemetery in Margraten* (Margraten: Stichting Akkers van Margraten, 2009); *Akkers van Margraten* (Ruim Kader Films, 2010).

That was sixty-five years after he had worked there as a gravedigger. He shook hands with many people while there and was astonished to learn that no one he met knew about the segregation of the US Army during World War II. That is why he asked me to help him write his recollections of that awful time. I did so in March 2010, at his home in Connecticut. His neighbor, Sherryl Hauck, a camerawoman, filmed the whole conversation we had – day by day. The transcription of her film in English was translated into Dutch and edited with the help of Janice Wiggins, Jeff's wife, after Jeff had passed away. The book was presented in November 2014.

This second English edition, expanded with information based on research conducted since then – with additions to Jeff's own words – was translated into English by Frans Kooymans. As to historical dates and facts, the book is based on Jeff's recollections. Facts presented in historical archives and other books do not necessarily have a greater impact than what Jeff remembered.

The original edition led to a follow-up oral history project entitled *Kinderen van zwarte bevrijders* (*Children of Black Liberators*) and to a book with the same title.* Owing in my opinion to the impact of the Black Lives Matter movement, this has since resulted in several new productions in the Netherlands about the role of Black American liberators during World War II.

While working on this second edition, I often watched

---

* Mieke Kirkels, *Kinderen van zwarte bevrijders. Een verzwegen geschiedenis* (Nijmegen: Vantilt, 2017).

the news on television about the war in Ukraine. Especially when mass graves and the transport and burial of slain soldiers were mentioned, I could only think of what Jeff Wiggins told me: History keeps repeating itself!

Mieke Kirkels, September 2024

Introduction to this Edition

> "Until the lion tells the story,
> the hunter will always be the hero"
> – African saying

> "As a very young, Black soldier in a segregated army, Jeff had no sense or concept of the fact that his place in history would even be noticed, much less that it would have any meaning or significance to anyone in the years to come."
> – Janice Wiggins

September 2009. My husband and I were boarding a plane for a trip to the past, a past that had been buried for sixty-five years. We were traveling to the Netherlands, to a place where Jeff had spent the most traumatic weeks of his army time in World War II, a place of kind people and unspeakable memories. We were traveling to Margraten.

Few Americans have ever heard of Margraten. Few historical accounts of World War II mention this village in the southernmost tip of the Netherlands, nestled quietly in the region between Belgium and Germany – a village that became the site of one of the largest American military cemeteries in Europe.

Our trip was born of Jeff's sense of duty, his sense of responsibility as the last known living member of a company of African American soldiers, who helped establish the Netherlands American Cemetery in Margraten. That

Jefferson Wiggins and his wife, Janice Paterson Wiggins, and General Egon Ramms, Commander of the NATO Joint Forces Command, in the Limburg town of Brunssum, during the Margraten Requiem Concert at the American Cemetery on September 13, 2009
(Photo: Felicia Wiggins)

sense of duty did not come without a price. It was a price that many soldiers pay as they manage or suppress memories of duties performed and tragedies confronted.

This book is a work of pain and honor, a commitment to tell a story that had never been told, a story seen through a lens that no one else could share anymore. It is the account of two hundred and sixty Black soldiers in a segregated army, who were given the horrific yet honorable job of burying white soldiers who had been killed in battle – white soldiers whom they were forbidden to join as equals in the battles of World War II. It captures Jeff's memories and thoughts as the last known living Black soldier of that unit when he returned to Margraten in 2009, at the invitation of the municipality of Margraten and the *Akkers van Margraten* oral history project, to celebrate the sixty-fifth anniversary of the liberation of the southern region of the Netherlands.

Jeff placed a high priority on completing this book and ensuring that history recorded the contribution of his company at Margraten, a record written from the perspective of one of their own. His health did not last long enough for him to finish this work, but his memories were captured in an interview with Mieke Kirkels in March 2010. We have used the filmed recording of that interview to fill in the spaces and finish the story that he considered so important to tell. My hope is that we have done justice to his wishes and have fulfilled his mission honorably.

Janice Wiggins
Connecticut, August 2014

Mieke Kirkels interviewing Jeff Wiggins, March 2010
(Photo: Sheryll Hauck)

Introduction to the Second Edition

> "History is not just facts and events. History is also a pain in the heart, and we repeat history until we are able to make another's pain in the heart ours."
> – Professor Julius Lester, born in St. Louis

Jeff Wiggins was in the Netherlands in 2009. He had been here before, as a soldier, during World War II. Back then he was one of hundreds of African American soldiers who arrived in Margraten in late 1944 to bury thousands of slain soldiers there. In 2009 he returned as one of the last surviving eyewitnesses of those days. Jeff Wiggins considered it his duty to tell the story of his experiences of those days.

Only since recently have stories about World War II arisen that are told from the perspective of African American soldiers. Jeff Wiggins wanted to add to these his personal recollections of the time that he spent in the US Army, where white and Black soldiers were strictly segregated from each other.

That was the reason he asked me, towards the end of his second stay in Limburg in 2009: "Do you want to do a project with me?" Whether I would help him record his

Jefferson Wiggins' grave in New Fairfield in 2015
(Photo: Mieke Kirkels)

recollections of his time in the US Army. I saw this as a great honor, as a responsible task, but also as a challenge to meet his request the way it should be.

In a long series of interview sessions at his home in March 2020, Jeff told me his story of World War II. They are the recollections of an exceptional man in an exceptional time of history. Together with Jeff, and ultimately with the help of his wife Janice, I put his experiences on paper.

The things Jeff mentioned were often disconcerting. His stories incited me to search for backgrounds and for precise details about the contribution of African Americans to the liberation of Europe. Jeff's experiences and insights are embedded in this book in their historical context.

In November 2014, when the first edition of this book

was just about finished, race riots in Ferguson, a suburb of St. Louis, Missouri, were frontpage news. The residents of Ferguson, mostly African Americans, were furious because white police officers had shot and killed Michael Brown, young Black man. It was hardly the first time that this happened because of someone's skin color. I wondered what Jeff's reaction to this would have been. In the book he responded to the everyday racism during his days in Margraten with the lament: "That's how it was in those days ... and sometimes still is today."

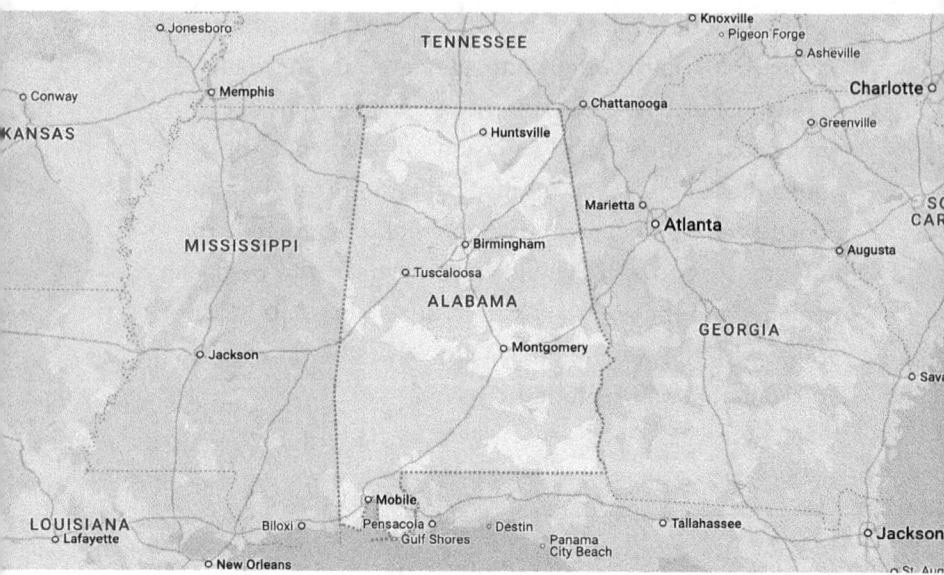

Alabama, where Jeff grew up, and surrounding states
(Source: Google Maps)

CHAPTER 1 – Houston County, Alabama

FROM BOY TO MAN IN A SINGLE DAY

January 1942. A Black teenager walks up the steps of the post office in Dothan, Alabama. The teenager, his name is Jeff, is the errand boy for the local drugstore. He holds a package in his hands, that he needs to deliver to Sergeant Faulkner, who has his office on the fourth floor of the building.

Jeff knocks on the door, hears "yes," opens it, and sees a tall blond man. This is Faulkner, a sergeant in the Marines. Jeff lays the package on his desk. Faulkner asks, "How much is it, boy?"* Jeff answers that the price is written on the package. "That is not what I asked," Faulkner says. "Can't you read, boy?"

---

* Nearly all African American men were called "boy" at that time, regardless of their age. That was not so in the army. Wiggins was called by his real name there from the very first day.

Jeff quickly turns around, but before he reaches the door, Faulkner tells him to wait. Jeff obviously does so and then hears: "Turn around. You're a big boy. Do you know that our country is at war?" Jeff knows that. Faulkner tells him that he looks a bit thin and that it would serve him well to enlist in the army. Jeff doesn't quite understand what the man is after. Faulkner asks, "Do you get enough to eat?" plus some more. Then he asks, "How old are you? Are you eighteen?" Jeff is not used to talking with white people. And he never thought about his age. He lives by the day. That doesn't involve thinking about the future.

Jeff: "Where my answer came from, I don't know, but I said, 'Yes, sir, eighteen,' even though that was a lie. I was about sixteen. I say 'about' because age back then was only approximate. Nowadays everyone knows the exact date of birth of a baby. Back then, a doctor or midwife did have to fill out forms for the Bureau of Vital Statistics, a sort of population register, but when a Black baby was born no one was in a hurry to do so. It might be as much as three months later when a birth was officially recorded, assuming that it wasn't forgotten. A sister of mine wasn't registered at all. She only found that out when she was eighteen, when she wanted to sign up for the army."

Jeff had never given any thought as to whether he wanted to enlist. Actually, he wasn't planning to do so at all. But that was exactly what the sergeant tried to get him to do. Jeff: "The only thing I wanted right then and there was to get away from the man as quickly as possible. I was scared, real scared."

A LITTLE WHITE LIE

Jeff stood nailed to the ground opposite the sergeant, whom he had lied to. Lied to a white person, to a sergeant. It had happened in an impulse.

Jeff: "Never lie, no matter what you've been up to. That was the motto of my grandma Dawson. She was an amazing person. A small woman, with only grade school education. Her father had lived in the days of slavery. She was tremendous. She had arranged that errand job for me. When I had to deliver that package to Faulkner, I had a year and a half in that job behind me.

We lived on a sprawling cotton plantation that involved working from dawn to dusk. Often there was not enough to eat. Hardly any opportunity to attend school, and certainly not at the time of harvest. So I was glad with my little job at the drugstore.

Enlisting in the army, that I definitely wasn't prepared for. I had only said what I said to Faulkner to get away from the man as quick as possible. Something that I thought he would want to hear. Still, I left the room with application forms that I had to fill out at home. The whole day the voice of Sergeant Faulkner echoed through my head, while riding my bike around town delivering packages. Had he really said 'three meals a day'? And that you'd be taken care of if you became ill? And that I'd also get paid twenty-one dollars a month? That was a pile of money.

At the end of the day I rode back to the drugstore. When I put my bike in front of the door, I caught on to a conversation among a group of white women. One of

Strange Fruit
(Source: www.zapiro.com)

them said something about 'a little white lie.' That it could do no harm to tell a little white lie for your own sake. So long as you didn't harm or hurt anyone. What I had told Faulkner about my age was exactly that, a little white lie. So I convinced myself that evening that it would be perfect to enlist in the army. At home I didn't say a word about that plan, for I knew that they wouldn't let me go."

As well as he could, Jeff filled out the application forms. He put his mother's signature behind her name. His father had never learned to write, so he put an X below his name. A few days after Jeff had handed the application forms to Sergeant Faulkner, he left the house early in the morning. He had told no one what he intended to do. Before the rest of the family woke up, he was already on his way to where, according to Faulkner, he needed to report. A bus stood ready there to take him to Montgomery. From there he was off to Fort Benning in Georgia for a medical screening. Hundreds of Black men got their army outfit in that army camp.

It was January 1942 when Jeff passed his medical screening. Five days later he left by train to Fort Bragg in North Carolina.

In a single day the anonymous boy had turned into a man with a name.

ABOLITION OF SLAVERY

> "All men are created equal. They are endowed by their Creator with certain unalienable rights."
> – Thomas Jefferson, Declaration of Independence, 1776

In 1808 the international slave trade was forbidden in the United States, although slaves could still be bought and sold. Fifty-five years later, in 1863, slavery was abolished, with the Emancipation Proclamation by President Abraham Lincoln. But that did not mean that African Americans now had the same rights as white Americans. The original US Constitution, enacted in 1789, did not say a word about voting rights. The first ten amendments to that Constitution, the Bill of Rights, allowed the individual states to determine who was entitled to vote. Such was the situation until after the Civil War (1861–1865).* This war was based on the conflict between the Northern states (the Union) and the Southern states (the Confederation). The Northern states increasingly regarded slavery as an institution to be rejected, while the Southern states were economically dependent on slavery and thus against its abolition.

After the Civil War, in 1865, all slaves were formally freed through the enactment of the Thirteenth Amendment to the Constitution. Every person who was born in the United States or naturalized as an American citizen also obtained civil rights through the Fourteenth Amendment (1868). The Fifteenth Amendment (1870) officially gave former slaves the right to vote. However, from that time, intimidation campaigns against African Americans increased enormously. Various states took both legal and illegal actions to exclude them from the voting booths.

---

* After the end of the Civil War in 1865, Black Codes were enacted, which seriously limited the rights of the former slaves. These set out, for example, what type of work they were allowed to do, whether they could resign from work, what property they could own. The Reconstruction Act of 1867 limited the effect of the Black Codes as it called upon all states to respect the Fourteenth Amendment and to grant voting rights to Black men. (Women could not vote in federal elections until 1920.) Reconstruction officially ended in 1877, after which the Southern states introduced discriminatory legislation. White supremacy thus grew again. Legislation was based on the concept of "separate but equal."

Not all measures were explicit, but in practice Black Americans living in the Southern states were excluded. By 1910 it was customary again in these states that only white men were allowed to vote. This practice continued until 1965, when the Voting Rights Act was enacted by the US Congress.

THE KU KLUX KLAN

> "Hate is learned behavior"
> – Jefferson Wiggins

Jeff was seven years old when the Wiggins family was confronted with the feared Ku Klux Klan. His father was alleged to have stolen a bale of cotton. The situation was as follows. When a harvest was finished, the workers received part of the proceeds as payment. That year the price of the cotton was too low in the eyes of the plantation owner. So he delayed selling the cotton bales until the price would go up. The workers did not get paid, and the Wiggins family suffered. Jeff's father Clem had begged his boss for a bale of cotton to tide him over, but he was met with refusal. Clem took a bale anyway, sold it, and the family had food again to eat. This was discovered: sufficient reason for a visit by the Klansmen with their hoods and long white robes.

Jeff: "I believe it was shortly after midnight when a group of some forty men approached our house. They walked back and forth in front of the house, carrying weapons. Grandma Dawson discovered it when she heard sounds that she didn't trust. She saw that the Klansmen had erected a large burning cross. She shut the door and woke my daddy. He left the house immediately through the back door.

From that moment on it was clear to us that we couldn't stay in our house anymore. We left quickly, because there was a big chance that the Klan would come back. If they weren't able to find my daddy, someone else might be lynched in his place. We left that same night to another county. We were afraid in the meantime that he had been abducted by the Klan. It happened more often that people just disappeared and were never heard from again. But after a few days he found us, and he stayed with us in our new home."

Jeff knew all too well what the Klan was up to. Every Black child knew that. The threat never went away. "Stick to the rules of the whites," that was the urgent message that Jeff received time and again from his father, mother, and older brothers and sisters. "If you don't, they'll make you pay, they'll kill you." He seldom talked about the Klan with his friends because you never knew who might be eavesdropping. At home, within the family, or at table the subject was discussed. Or on Sunday, on the way to church. And when the family went grocery shopping on Saturday afternoon in town, the children were instructed beforehand how to behave.

Jeff: "In those days, if you ran into a white person, you had to step off the sidewalk and continue on in the street.

Never stay on the same sidewalk with whites. That sort of thing you just knew. Our parents had hammered the Klan rules into our brains. Of course, we were pissed about it, but what could we do? We lived with a laugh and a tear, between hope and fear. We wouldn't dream of making jokes about the men with their eerie white robes and hoods. If you talked about the Klan at all, it was whispering. Nobody knew who might be a member. In church, the minister might mention it at times, but only in covert ways. And never show that you were indignant about it, for that could have serious consequences."

Until the time when the Klan came to their house to get hold of his father, Jeff had never seen their rituals. Sometimes he did encounter them in their robes, carrying rifles. And on Saturdays they might walk up and down the streets. They were the boss, that was the unmistakable message.

ORIGINS OF THE KU KLUX KLAN

After 1808, when the international slave trade was officially banned, slaves could be ransomed. At the end of the Civil War, in 1865, when all slaves had been declared free, opponents responded with the establishment of the Ku Klux Klan (KKK), in Pulaski, Tennessee. By 1870, the KKK had chapters in all Southern states. Originally it was a secret organization, which focused in particular on threats and intimidation of the so-called Freedmen, the liberated slaves. The goal was to have the Freedmen abandon their newly acquired rights. In 1871 the US Congress enacted the

Ku Klux Klan Act, whereafter President Ulysses S. Grant took sturdy action against the Klan, in particular in South Carolina. Although prosecutions led to relatively few convictions, the impact was such that the KKK practically ceased to exist by 1872. Meanwhile, however, several Southern states enacted so-called Black Codes, which restricted the rights of African Americans and were meant to ensure that cheap Black labor was still available even after the abolition of slavery.

After the Reconstruction period, which ended in 1877 when the Democrats regained power in the South, laws were introduced that went even further. The name Jim Crow became associated with these discriminatory laws, which were enacted to maintain racial segregation. A few examples: mixed marriages were forbidden, and employers were required to keep Black and white personnel separated. In 1896, in the Plessy v. Ferguson case, the Supreme Court ruled that such laws were constitutional: "separate but equal." In addition, a new KKK organization was established in 1915 in Atlanta. This time the Klan aimed also at other groups, such as Jews, Catholics, Communists, Immigrants, and trade union members. At its zenith in the 1920s, the Klan had more than four million members. In 1944 the organization was officially dissolved, but it remained active in secret until the 1960s, when the civil rights movement emerged. In 1965, President Lyndon Johnson openly condemned the Klan. Still, in the 1990s the Klan had some ten thousand active members in the Southern states. By 2021 the number of groups that identified themselves with the Ku Klux Klan had dwindled to twenty. However, the total number of white nationalist groups in the country today is a multiple of these.*

ENLIST OR BE DRAFTED?

For the United States, World War II started on December 7, 1941, the day after Pearl Harbor was bombed by the Japanese.** Large contingents of American soldiers headed for Europe and other parts of the world for war service, including many Blacks, but fully segregated from their white compatriots. Altogether, more than a million African

---

* The Jim Crow laws, which stayed in force in the Southern states for nearly a century, were meant to minimize the position of African Americans, such as by denying them the right to vote and excluding them from education. Until the Civil Rights Act of 1964, discrimination and racial segregation were legal. Theaters, hotels, and restaurants were strictly segregated, and in stores blacks were served last. In 1954 the Supreme Court finally declared discrimination in education to be unconstitutional, but it took another ten years before minorities got full equal rights. To this day, the term Jim Crow is used in the US to refer to legislation and customs that discriminate African Americans.

** The massive strike on the naval base of Pearl Harbor in Hawaii on December 7, 1941 was a surprise attack by the Japanese imperial navy under the leadership of Admiral Isoroku Yamamoto. The attack was meant to destroy most of the US fleet so that Japan would have total control in the Pacific Ocean. It was a tremendous shock to the American nation and led directly to the involvement of the United States in World War II, both in the Pacific and in Europe. The day after the attack the US declared war on Japan. During the attack on Pearl Harbor, 1,402 Americans died and 1,182 were wounded. The losses the Japanese suffered were much smaller, with a mere 65 killed or wounded and one Japanese sailor taken prisoner.

Americans took part in World War II, with nine hundred thousand of these serving in Europe.

Jeff: "Most Black Americans in the army were draftees. But there were also quite a few who, just like me, enlisted in the armed forces voluntarily. They had signed up because of circumstances back home: humiliation, hunger, poverty, lack of medical care. As an army volunteer you at least got enough to eat, three meals a day. You could expect good medical care, and with a bit of luck you'd be treated more respectfully than back home. But did we also go to help out? For love of our country? The place names that we heard on the radio meant nothing to us. We had no idea where they were exactly. Today I'd put it like this: choosing to enlist in the army was, for many, a mix of loyalty towards our country and loyalty towards yourself.

But, loyalty to our country? As for me, I had no idea really as to what that could entail. I'd had little opportunity to go to school, but the few times that I went, we had to sing this famous patriotic song: *My country 'tis of thee, Sweet land of liberty ... Land of the pilgrims' pride ... land where my father died ...* My father had almost died, but for another reason. It didn't feel real good to sing: *This is my country.**

When I entered the army, I was totally prepared to carry out every assignment. I was smart enough to realize that circumstances at home were damned bad. Still, I was

---

* The lyrics of *My Country, 'Tis of Thee* (a de-facto national anthem before the adoption of *The Star-Spangled Banner* as the official anthem in 1931) were altered several times over time. Jeff included lines from the abolitionist version.

Jeff as a young soldier during military training in 1944. Front row, third from right (Source: Wiggins collection)

convinced, without exactly knowing how, that that situation would change by me going into the army. And that was the case.

In the army, we young Black Americans often talked about the miserable conditions back home. But when you asked someone else whether they had volunteered or were drafted, most of them said that they were draftees. You knew they were lying. Most of them had freely enlisted. But that was hard to admit, after you had been suppressed, ignored, and treated as a second-rate citizen your entire life. A question of pride. We were not always treated fairly. And yet, if I had been asked back then whether I wanted to be an American or something else, I would have chosen to be American. And many along with me. That I am convinced of."

ARMY SERVICE AND SLAVERY

During the Civil War, the former slave Robert Smalls, who later became a politician and was elected to the South Carolina legislature, gained freedom. He had been the first African American to serve as captain with the Marines. After that war, some African American leaders thought it was to the benefit of the Black community to join the armed forces and show bravery and dedication to the nation. During the American revolutionary war, five thousand African Americans had fought along with the colonists. But by the time of the Japanese attack against the United States at Pearl Harbor, on December 7, 1941, the memories of the heroic feats of the two hundred thousand African Americans who had fought during the Civil War and later wars had faded.

During World War II, the US was in dire need of soldiers. Because of this, in addition to draftees being called up for military service, volunteers were recruited until late 1942 among the Black population to join the war effort. They were good soldiers, but they only worked in support functions, such as that of tailor, cook, gravedigger, or truck driver. Also, they transported ammunition to the troops. The combat troops and officers were white. The Black-white relationship in army and air force was then about 20 to 80 in percentage terms.

Because of the racial segregation in the US, white and Black American military personnel were placed in separate army units. People who never talked to each other in civilian life, who could not sit together in the same room, who did not know each other and even regarded each other as "the enemy," how would they be able to work together effectively? It had been tried, but it turned out to be difficult. What also played a role is that Black Americans were considered mentally inferior when it came to dealing with weapons. Worse even, they were not trusted with a weapon in their hand.

Jeff: "I was fully aware that racial segregation existed not just at home but also in the army. Black and white had always lived separately in the various states. In Alabama, the state that I came from, the situation was worst. For me, anything was better than that, even a segregated army. But all of us waited for the time when someone, in whatever way, would bring change to the situation."

AFRICAN AMERICANS IN THE TWO WORLD WARS

In World War I, some 400,000 African Americans were involved in the American army. Former slave owners were compensated for that. In World War II more than 1.2 million African Americans served in the military. That involved the home front, Europe, and the Pacific War. That number included 6,500 members of the Women's Army Corps (WAC), the female support troops.

Altogether, 125,000 African American men and women took part in World War II, 6.25% of all US soldiers in Europe and the Pacific, and 16.000 were stationed in the Netherlands. 708 of them died during the war. Of these, 169 are buried in Margraten, and the names of three missing African American soldiers are mentioned on the Wall of the Missing.

RECRUITMENT

Jeff: "My first training period was at Fort Bragg in Georgia. After that came Camp Philips in Kansas. The interview I had there I still remember vividly. After the first training I was appointed as staff sergeant. The captain who was going to lead our unit could select candidates from the volunteers. He conducted the interviews with two other officers and must have spoken to hundreds of men. The first thing he asked me was why I wanted to join the 960th Quartermaster Service Company (QMSC). I answered that it was not up to me to choose the 960th, but up to the 960th to choose me or not. One of the officers asked: 'Do you think you might be too good for the 960th?' 'No,' I said, 'but I do understand that, when you're in the army, it's the army that decides where you go.'

Today I have to laugh at my cocky answer of back then! After the interview I didn't trust it at all. I thought I had really messed up. But I was wrong. A few days later I got word that I would be part of the 960th QMSC. Before we left for Europe, our unit was complete, consisting of 260 Black soldiers. We knew that it wouldn't be a combat unit, but we had no idea what our tasks would consist of. During the months that followed, we were drilled and trained. We learned all sorts of things about safety tasks, about patrolling during the night, and about setting up a tent camp."

Next, the 960th was stationed in Camp Shanks in New York State and thereafter in Fort Wadsworth on Staten Island. There Jeff was in training for twelve weeks. He became company clerk, reporting directly to the first sergeant. The soldiers would later leave New York State in thousands, for the ocean crossing to Europe. But whether Jeff would be among them remained uncertain. All because he had lied about his age.

AN UNEXPECTED RENDEZVOUS WITH MOTHER ESSIE
Jeff: "Not long after I started military service, I read something that scared me enormously. We had to study the Uniform Code of Military Justice, the military laws and regulations. In a certain article it said that anyone who had not told the truth when applying, who had lied about his age, or concealed a criminal record, would have to appear before a military tribunal. In case of conviction, that would mean a five-year prison sentence. I panicked because I really feared ending up in a military prison as a criminal. That particular article was, after all, about me: I had lied about my age. A Bible text that my mother often quoted came to mind: 'You shall know the truth, and the truth will save you.' I decided that the best thing to do was to admit my lie to the military leadership. Initially no one believed

me, but I provided the name of someone in my birth town who knew my parents and who was certain to have a telephone. My courage failed me, but I had no other choice. The fear of being sent back to Alabama was greater than the fear of a prison term!"

Because he was not even eighteen yet, Jeff could only stay in the army – and that would be highly exceptional – if his parents gave permission. When they heard this, his mother traveled all the way from Alabama to New York. Her only objective was to take her son, who had suddenly disappeared two years ago, back home with her.

When she arrived at the military barracks and finally saw Jeff again, they fell into each other's arms in tears. Jeff held onto her as if his life depended on it. In a certain sense it felt that way. Mother Essie was extremely happy that he was still alive and was doing well. She was amazed to see how healthy he looked. She said, "If I had run into you in the street, I wouldn't have recognized you."

Jeff tried to explain to her why he had left home, but his mother wouldn't listen. "When we get home, we'll have enough time to discuss that." But that was not what Joff had in mind, to go home. He definitely wanted her to understand why he felt at home in the army. One of the main reasons was that he had never been called nigger or boy by anyone during his two years in the army. Here he had a name, he was somebody. He didn't want to go back home, where he would once again be a nobody and be called "boy."

Lots of talks followed with army officials, with an army

Mother Essie (Source: Wiggins collection)

chaplain, and with his mother. Even a general got involved. His mother wouldn't budge, did not accept that Jeff would stay in the army. And Jeff? He seriously doubted that he could still live in Alabama after all that he had experienced and learned in the past two years.

In the end, Jeff managed to get everyone to agree that he could stay in the army. He succeeded in convincing not just his superiors, but also his mother. After all, as a soldier he could do more for his family than by going back to Alabama. Plus, staying in Alabama was no option for him at all, Jeff emphasized, "no matter what." Regardless of whether she'd force him to go back, no way would he stay at home. "I may have to go back, but I don't have to stay."

Jeff's age was then corrected in the military records. After the necessary formalities, his mother had to sign an official document, stating that she did not object to her seventeen-year-old son staying in the army.

Shortly before his mother traveled back to Alabama, Jeff handed her the money that he had saved from his military pay all this time. He said goodbye in the barracks. The chaplain had convinced them that the departure would be less emotional for them if Jeff were to see his mother off at the train station. From that time on, Jeff regularly wrote to his family and transferred money.

TRAINING BEFORE DEPARTURE FOR EUROPE

The war brought lots of changes to the American army. One of the changes concerned policies with regard to leadership functions. There were simply not enough professional soldiers to meet the growing demand for supervisory personnel. For that reason, younger soldiers, such as Jeff, got leading positions earlier than they would have in the past. Shortly after his eighteenth birthday, on February 22, 1943, Jeff was promoted to the position of staff sergeant.

Jeff: "When our staff sergeant got wounded during a

training session, there was suddenly the need for someone to take his place. You need to realize that at that time the average age of a staff sergeant in the US army was between 40 and 45. And there I was, just eighteen and far from certain in lots of things. One advantage of war – if you can call that an advantage – is that you grow to adulthood fast, real fast. I was quite aware that most of the men I had under me were older than me. I often wondered what they thought of that. But it all went well."

A FRIENDSHIP IN THE LIBRARY

While awaiting passage to Europe, Jeff was stationed in Fort Wadsworth on Staten Island, New York. One day he got to talking to one of his officers. The conversation was about the lack of proper schooling, and Jeff asked: "Where would you go if you want to learn things?" The answer he got was: "To the library." On his next day off Jeff headed for the nearest library, Stapleton Library, not far from the army camp. From that time on, he was to be found there regularly. Back home, in Alabama, he had never been to a library. That was *for whites only*. But in New York, at his first visit to this library he was welcomed by one of the staffers, Mrs. Merrill. She asked him what book he was looking for. That was the start of a long friendship. Jeff had barely completed grade school in Alabama. He could read some, because his mother had taught him and his siblings to read the Bible. He had also gotten some lessons from a retired teacher, in exchange for maintaining his garden. Mrs. Merrill not only told Jeff the ins and outs of the library

Stapleton Branch Library in 1940 (Courtesy of NYPL image Gallery. www.NYPL.org)

but also tutored him and discussed all sorts of subjects, such as society, the war in Europe, and the situation of African Americans in the US. With her help, Jeff managed a big catchup in his knowledge and social development in several months. She gave him a feeling of self-esteem.

Because of the positive impression that Jeff had left with the military leadership, such as by confessing his true age, he received special study facilities before his departure for Europe. As often as his training schedule allowed, he was brought to the library on an army motor. Jeff: "During that time I didn't socialize much with the other soldiers. I studied and read a lot and wrote letters to my folks back home. A few of the guys in my unit complained that I kept too much to myself. That I had become a snob. But I don't think I was like that. I just realized how much I still had to learn."

A BLACK ARMY AND A WHITE ARMY

Before the departure for Europe, the US in fact had two armies. The combat units were almost entirely white. Black Americans constituted the support troops, the Quartermaster Service Companies. They handled supporting services and consisted almost entirely of Black soldiers. Only the officers were white. The QMSCs in turn were part of the Quartermaster Corps, the QMC.

Jeff was part of the 960th QMSC. With 260 soldiers and various officers this was a relatively large company.

Jeff: "If I were to explain to my great-grandson Malcolm or any other school kids of his age why there were two armies, I would first of all explain that our country never overcame the transatlantic slave trade, that it never overcame the fact that, somewhere along the African coast, European trading companies bribed African chiefs to capture Black people and took these on board of their ships. That they were transported to North America and the Caribbean under brutal conditions and sold to slave traders and plantation owners.*

---

* Exact figures regarding the slave trade are not available. Estimates range from 10 to 21 million people who were taken from Africa to North and South America. About half a million of these were transported by Dutch ships. The Dutch share in the international slave trade thus came to roughly five percent, with the Westindische Compagnie and the Middelburgsche Commercie Compagnie as the main participants in that

Just imagine what happens when someone is taken captive. The person imprisoned is from that moment subordinated to whoever makes him prisoner. The captive has no say whatsoever. From the moment that these Africans set foot on our shores, they were regarded as inferior. That's what happened in the sixteenth and seventeenth centuries, and the effects of it we experience to this very day."

trade. Portugal was by far the largest slave trader, as it was responsible for taking some 46 percent of all African slaves taken across the Atlantic Ocean. Second in line were the British, with 26 percent. Then came France and Denmark, with 13 and 8 percent, respectively. Source: interview Jefferson Wiggins by Mieke Kirkels CT, March 2010.

CHAPTER 2 – A Segregated Crossing to Scotland

The 960th QMSC was established in Camp Phillips in Kansas in 1943. On February 27, 1944 the company left from New York to Glasgow, Scotland, where it arrived two weeks later, on March 11.

Jeff: "We left for Europe from the Staten Island Terminal and Port of Embarkation in New York. The ship, the Frederick Lykes, set course for Scotland. The crossing took much longer than foreseen, and not just because it was wartime. There were over two thousand men on board. Black and white were strictly separated. Black troops were kept below deck, white troops were on the upper deck. Conditions in the lower parts of the ship were clearly less comfortable than above. The upper parts had windows, whereas it was stuffy below.

The days on board were not structured very tightly, and we were free to walk on deck if we wanted to. Quite a few soldiers got seasick, Black as well as white. There were several quite scary moments, such as on the third day of the crossing, when the ship's rudder turned out to be defective. For three days we floated around in that big tub, adrift among the high waves. We were scared of those waves, but much more so of German submarines. We had heard that they caused troop ships as well as freight carriers to sink. Those were stressful days, believe me! After the rudder was replaced, we could finally go on again."

The circumstances on board were therefore quite different for Black and white soldiers. The lower you got in the ship, the less comfortable it was. It was hot there. In our section of the ship, there were two large ventilators, as I recall. Our company had two decks: one in the bottom of the ship, the other one right above it. No windows whatsoever. Still we were treated equally, as much as was possible under the circumstances. There was hardly any contact between the Black and white soldiers while on board. But we knew that, as soon as we arrived on the battlefield, the exploding shells and bombs would make no distinction between Black and white.

There was a recreation deck, with lounges and various relaxation facilities that we were not allowed to use. Nothing like that on our deck. Soldiers were known to be big gamblers, with cards and dice and such. Downstairs a corner was quickly arranged for the card players and another one for the dice players. There was also a special corner for church services. Another part, the most popular one, was for gospel singers. I loved to sing."

WAR IS THE ULTIMATE EQUALIZER

Jeff: "The gospel corner came about by accident more or less. Two of our soldiers had gotten into a fight with each other and were therefore locked up. Not long after the fight we heard singing coming from the hold where they were put away. To our surprise it was the two of them who were singing! They were both excellent singers. They continued singing after they were back with us. Everyone was quite impressed. They were the best singers we had heard. I remember the name of one of them, Archie Johnson. His former rival was a soldier from Wheeling in West Virginia, but I can't come up with his name now. From that day on, quite a few soldiers regularly gathered around the two when they started singing. Even inveterate gamblers quit their activities to listen to the soothing, beautiful music. After a while a growing number of white soldiers also came down. Everyone, whether religious or not, seemed to suddenly turn into a believer in those days. Each of us was afraid not to survive the war. That may well have been the background to this.

A couple of songs were favorite. Archie Johnson loved to sing *Coming home, coming home, Lord, I'm coming home.* My own favorite was *Stand by me*, which became famous in the version sung by Tennessee Ernie Ford: *When I'm growing old and feeble, stand by me. When my life becomes a burden and I'm crossing chilly Jordan, thou who knowest all about me, stand by me.*

That, I believe, was the most popular song on board. The white soldiers knew, just like us, that they shouldn't be there. But we all knew too that, once in Europe, we'd be in the same predicament. War is the ultimate equalizer."

HEADS TURNING IN BRITAIN
Jeff: "We arrived in Scotland about three months before the Normandy invasion. After the ship docked, the white soldiers could leave first, to prepare living quarters. We, the Black soldiers, had to stay another night on the ship. We were relieved when we finally could come on shore and felt firm ground under our feet. At the same time, we wondered how close the Germans had gotten to Scotland and whether any bombs had fallen there. Fortunately, that was not case, quite a relief to us, at least for the time being. For our first night on land we were taken to a large field where we pitched small tents for a temporary camp. After a couple of nights there we were housed in a school building, where we stayed until our departure by train for Westbury in Wiltshire. The soldiers were housed in barracks there, the officers in rental houses. The commander of our company, Captain Raymond Kelms, notified his superiors that there were not enough recreational facilities in Scotland for the troops, except for a single room where the soldiers could on occasion get a beer. He also wrote that the cooks had trouble managing the British field kitchens. A bigger problem was that the non-commissioned officers, the NCOs, had fewer years of service than the mostly older professional soldiers that they were in charge of. Still, we were happy with the work, which mostly consisted of provisioning. The commander of depot G-47, where

we were put to work, praised our good work in a letter.

Once we were in Britain, we were surprised that people left their houses to stare at us when we marched through the streets. Except for the aristocrats who had spent time in the British colonies, few British men had ever seen Black people. We knew that stories went around where we were portrayed as wild beasts. It was also said that we could not be trusted and that it was better not to get too close to us. But now they left their houses in large numbers to gape at us. We were again confronted with the bizarre stories about Blacks and the theories that we were hardly human beings. Whether our captain ever knew that we were regarded that way, I don't know, but if so he never let us notice it. That would have been quite demoralizing, I'm sure.

We could go into town if we wanted. In fact, during my stay in Southern England, I went off to London a couple of times. Our captain tried to direct us to bars where hardly any white soldiers came. He knew all too well that otherwise there might be trouble."

BEER IN BIRMINGHAM

Jeff: "One day that I was off I visited Birmingham on my own. My captain had suggested this as it would be an interesting visit for me. I had heard of Birmingham in Alabama, but not of this Birmingham. It was an industrial city. At the very moment when the train arrived at the station, a few army units from the Islands arrived.* I saw that only

---

* The Islands usually refers to the British islands in the Caribbean area.

a few Black men and women were among them. We knew that the people from the West Indies were afraid of us, just like the white soldiers. They thought that their level of civilization was higher than that of American Blacks.

That day in Birmingham, while walking around all by myself, I was afraid of nothing. I probably had a misplaced feeling of security, such as: I am American and no one can hurt me. The train on which I rode had long wooden benches. I had one all to myself. Thinking back to that trip, it might well have been that no one wanted to sit next to me because in their eyes I was dangerous. In Birmingham itself I had no problem whatsoever, not even when I stepped into a pub. The beer, by the way, was the worst that I have ever tasted in my life. Just awful. It was maybe for the better, because I could have sat there the whole day and gotten stone drunk. After all, the people in the pub were surprisingly friendly."

LANDING IN NORMANDY

Anxiety increased as the 960th crossed the Channel from England to France.

Jeff: "Lots of jokes were told on board, mainly to break the tension. I remember that a soldier said to another: 'You see that white soldier there, and the Black one there? One of the two will not survive.' He was practically right. During war, death will get hold of you not because you are Black or white, but because you happen to be in the wrong place at the wrong time.

About an hour before we were to land, a soldier came

up to me. He was in his late forties. He asked me, 'Sergeant, are you afraid?' I answered, 'Sure, I'm afraid of death. How about you?' He hesitated, then said that he was afraid to die. 'Well,' I said, 'you are not the only one. All of these thousands are just as afraid to die as you. Maybe we are safer because of all those men who are afraid to die, just like us.'"*

---

* During the sixtieth anniversary of D-Day in 2004, no mention was made of African Americans at a special exhibition in Normandy. This struck Marine-Alice Mills, who knew of many friendships between French women and African American soldiers but saw nothing of this being referred to in the exhibition. She therefore collected stories of many people who were young in 1944–1945 and reconstructed the view that was presented in French school books. These spoke of "terror by Black soldiers in Normandy." In 2007 there was even a documentary entitled *The Neglected Story of African Americans on D-Day*, which contrasted altogether with the stories that Ms. Mills had collected. On the contrary, the exhibition at the celebration of D-Day in 2009 included photos that evidenced the good contacts between the French and the African Americans. The French media gave much attention to the new facts. Nevertheless, a book about D-Day published in 2013 contained a chapter about a large group of African Americans who had been stationed in Normandy for a long time, entitled "*Terreur noire dans le Bocage*" (Black Terror in Bocage, a central region in France). A stubborn stereotype, nearly seventy years after the fact. To counter this, Martine-Alice Mills wrote *Black GIs, Normandy 1944*, published in 2014: Martine-Alice Mills, *Soldats américains noirs, Normandie 1944/Black GIs, Normandy 1944* (Chassignol: Cahiers du Temps, 2014). She based this on interviews that she had held between 2004 and 2009 with eyewitnesses of that time. During the D-Day commemoration in 2014 a large group of American veterans was present as honorary guests, but not a single African American was among then. The next year saw the publication of *Forgotten: The Untold Story of D-Day's Black Heroes, at Home and at War* (New York and London: HarperCollins, 2015) by the French-American author Linda Hervieux. See also Linda Hervieux, "D-Day," *New York Daily*

HELL ON EARTH

Jeff: "The long wait before we got to the beach was plain awful. We had dropped anchor about a half mile from the beach and waited there for the landing crafts. These included amphibian crafts, open square vessels that could move through water at thirty to forty miles per hour. They were to pick us up to bring us from the ship to the beach. If you've ever been to Normandy, you're bound to know what it's like there. The beaches start out flat, but then you hit upon steep dunes. We saw that, but we also saw the bunkers on top of the dunes. Concrete blocks, reinforced with steel. Simply awesome."

THE COMPANY STAYS INTACT

Jeff: "Infantry troops preceded us into the dunes. Later, in the dark, you could hear the 'crickets,' small clicking devices used for sending messages. The infantry troops had those, each unit using its own signal. Everyone knew how many clicks it took to let your comrades know where you were. But we didn't have them, not being part of the combat troops.

Fortunately, most of us managed to find each other. But about eight of the 260 men of our company we couldn't find. That immediately led to jokes being made. Such as

News, June 5, 2009; Joseph Bamat, Joseph, "The Neglected Story of African Americans on D-Day," *France 24*, June 4, 2014, https://www.france24.com/en/20140604-d-day-african-american-battalion-320th-france-scholar-mills-dabney-normandy; and Jim Maceda, "Small Norman Village Honors Fallen Heroes," *NBC*, June 5, 2004, https://www.nbcnews.com/id/wbna5138079.

The invasion of Normandy, June 1942 (Source: Wikipedia)

that they had discovered that there was excellent wine in Normandy, enticing them to go after it. All clearly because of the tension. But we all thought and hoped that they were wounded and maybe taken to one of the hospital ships that lay in the Channel. From there they would be taken back to England. We had no idea.

The next day, late in the afternoon, the last ones finally joined us again. Luckily, no one was wounded or killed, which we had feared. They were discovered by a white unit, which brought them back to us. A great relief for us all."

The 320th Barrage Balloon Battalion, made up of Black soldiers, whose task was to prevent German aircraft from reaching the beaches (Source: Wikipedia)

HEADING TOWARDS BELGIUM

Two weeks after arriving in France, Jeff and his company started on the long journey inland, towards Paris. But the 960th QSMC never arrived there as instructions were altered several times along the way.

Jeff: "We passed, for example, through the totally destroyed city of Saint-Lô. The entire population was evacuated after the French underground had warned the city officials that an invasion was imminent." According to Jeff, the city was one large ruin. It had been totally bombed, first by Americans and British (on June 6 and 7, 1944), then also by Germans during Operation Cobra (July 25, 1944).

Jeff: "Not a single house was still intact. Even the church was totally destroyed. Earlier, thousands of people must have lived there. At first, all we saw were ruined buildings. Still, we saw inhabitants, for while we passed through the streets full of rubble, people came outside from the remnants of their homes. They had lost all their possessions, and still they were jubilant, glad that the Germans had left.

One of the most memorable encounters that I had in Europe was there, with a middle-aged woman. She came out of the hills with several bottles of French wine and Calvados in her backpack. Good stuff! She handed them out to the soldiers who passed by. She said to me, 'Soldier, you have no idea how it is to lose your freedom and what it means to get it back.' That touched me tremendously, because it made me realize what I had missed all my life. If I had had enough time and if my French had been better, I would have answered, 'Lady, you have no idea how it is to have never known freedom.' So there I was, somewhere in the middle of a country that I had never been to before, risking my life. I marched through a city that I knew nothing about and spoke with a woman that I would probably never see again. I saw how she celebrated freedom. Freedom that I should be entitled to back home, but which I didn't get. I'll never forget that moment in France."

On September 28, the 960th left by army truck for Le Mans. The next day they went to Lèves, where they stayed until October 21. The journey then continued by train, to Boirs in Belgium, near Liège, where they arrived on October 24. Five days later they arrived "somewhere in Belgium," according to Jeff.

NO GUN, NO LIBERATOR

Jeff: "After we had left Normandy and passed through Saint-Lô, the war developed much faster than anyone expected. We moved towards Liège in Belgium. While the people there were friendlier than in Britain and parts of France, we were still not exactly welcomed with open arms. Maybe the population reacted a bit uneasy because they had never seen Blacks before. But when we entered a store or a bar, people were friendlier toward us. And obviously they got even friendlier the more we drank. The way we were received in Belgium was possibly one of the first signs that something was changing regarding us, Black soldiers.

What I obviously don't know, or even doubt, is whether Belgians, the French, and the British regarded us as true equals of the whites. Our role in the liberation was clearly appreciated, but if you didn't have a gun, then you couldn't be a real liberator. If you were a Black soldier who had to supply other soldiers, had to dig graves, and bury bodies, or did other work that they didn't have to do, then they might be grateful towards you. But that didn't make you a liberator.

It was hardly surprising that the white part of the army got far greater attention after the war. It is not lack of respect that I say this, and I don't say it due to hard feelings, but that is simply how it was in those days. That all gradually changed during and due to the war."*

---

* Historian Peter Schrijvers has described the Belgian reaction to the arrival of African American troops in 1944/45 as follows: "The Belgians were astonished at seeing countless blacks in American uniforms. The nation had ruled for decades over millions of blacks in Congo, but the *Heart of Darkness* [title of the book by Joseph Conrad] had been very remote for most. Hardly any Africans lived in Belgium at the time, and the picture that government and church institutions had presented of the subjected natives in the colony had created the image of a primitive people that hungered for advance to civilization. The Belgian reactions to the first black GIs could have easily been those of the first European medieval explorers to set foot on the African continent [...]. It was quite a revelation to see how the image of dark natives who were in urgent need of civilization was blown up by black liberators in neat uniforms at the wheel of jeeps." (Peter Schrijvers, *De Margraten boys. Hoe een dorp weigerde de Amerikaanse bevrijders te vergeten* [Antwerp: Manteau, 2012], pp. 17 and 19.)

CHAPTER 3 – Digging Graves

On September 12, 1944 the first American soldier crossed the Dutch border from Belgium near Mesch, while at the same time fighting with German army units was still ongoing. The soldiers who died in this area were buried in the Belgian towns of Fosse (near Namur) and Henri-Chapelle (not far from Margraten). Immediately thereafter a start was made with the development of an American cemetery in Margraten.

Jeff: "At a given moment, somewhere in Belgium, Liège maybe, we heard of our new assignment. That was not until the evening before we had to report at the next location. Our captain called us: 'We are leaving tomorrow, so I want the entire unit to be ready on time.' When I asked where we were going, he answered, 'You'll hear that when the time comes.' We had arrived there around nine in the evening, I believe. We got into our sleeping bags.

After a three-hour ride or so in our trucks the next day,

we got to the village of Gronsveld. There we were quartered in a school, while the staff of our company stayed in the adjacent castle. Till last year I always thought that this village was somewhere in Belgium. But it turns out to lie on the Dutch side of the Meuse, on the other side of the border, in the southernmost part of the Netherlands, which had just been liberated. Gronsveld lies close to Margraten."*

WHY A VILLAGE IN SOUTHERN LIMBURG?

Right after the liberation of Southern Limburg, Captain Joseph James Shomon of the 611th Graves Registration Company (GRC) was assigned by General William Hood Simpson with the task of finding a suitable area for an American cemetery as quickly as possible.** The general had promised the soldiers of the Ninth Army that, should they die, they would not be buried in enemy territory.

Shomon originally opted for a location near Sittard, but that was too close to enemy lines. So he looked for a site

---

* According to military records, the 960th arrived in Margraten on October 29, 1944, after it had spent two weeks on what is nowadays the Chemelot plant in Heerlen. From there it went towards Gronsveld. (Source: archive Regionaal Historisch Centrum Limburg)

** Captain Joseph James Shomon was commander of the 611th Graves Registration Company and served in Europe for two years. From September 1944 he was in charge of the construction of the American cemetery in Margraten. He wrote *Crosses in the Wind*, an autobiographical account of his time in Europe during World War II: Joseph Shomon, *Crosses in the Wind: Graves Registration Service in the Second World War* (New York: Stratford House, 1947).

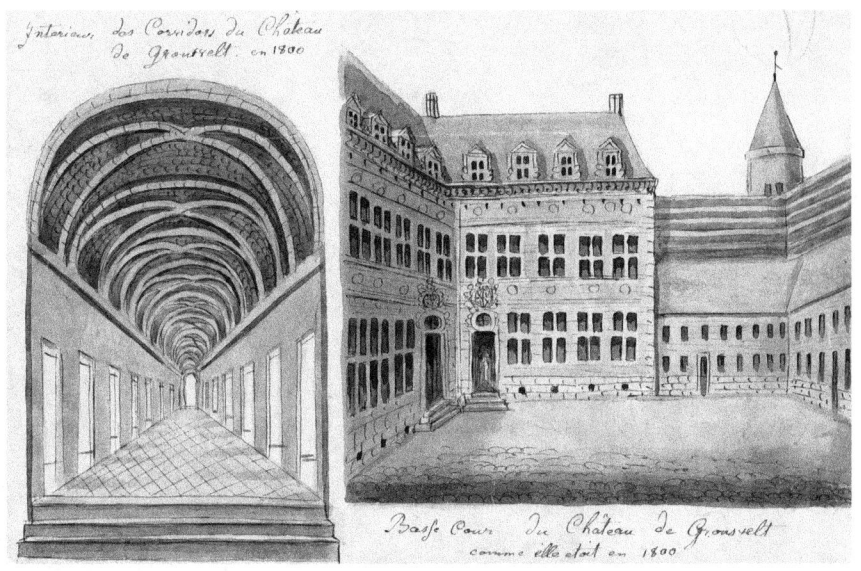

Gronsveld Castle, where officers of the 960th QMSC were quartered (Source: Samenwerkende Heemkunde Organisaties Margraten – SHOM)

further south. That is when he came across Margraten, because of the favorable location next to the main road that ran right across Southern Limburg. This encompassed all of 26 hectares, some 64 acres. The 611th GRC started work in the farming village of Margraten, which had a population of merely 1,200 back then. Soldiers' bodies were brought there in convoys from various battlefields and emergency cemeteries.

The elementary school in Gronsveld, where Wiggins was quartered with his company (Source: SHOM)

THE GRAVES REGISTRATION COMPANY

As troops advanced to do battle with German army units, trucks of the Graves Registration Company (GRC) rode along. During the fighting this company had the task of preparing a mass grave near the battlefield and later burying all those killed there, including German casualties and civilians. That was done out of respect but especially because it would be demotivating for the troops to see bodies lying by the road. The exact location of these temporary graves was recorded meticulously. As the establishment of the Margraten cemetery progressed, those who had fallen were taken there for their final resting place.

Soldiers stationed in the store owned by Dominique van den Bergh, Sittard, 1944–1945 (Photo: Dominique van den Bergh)

From September 1944 to June 1945 the work at Margraten was carried out under the leadership of Captain Shomon, first by the 611th and later by the 603rd GRC. The very first grave digging was done by the 3136th QMSC, which stayed in Margraten for a longer period. The 960th QMSC worked at the cemetery from November 17 until December 18, 1944. Dutch men also joined the work later, on a voluntary or paid basis, to bury the many bodies. After the repatriation of many dead soldiers back to the US in consultation with their families, the remaining bodies were reburied.

German prisoners of war built field laboratories. These

Dead awaiting burial (Source: US Army Archives)

were used to try to determine the identity of all unknown Americans who had died in Europe.

Soldier Dead by Michael Sledge is regarded as the standard reference work about the way US soldiers who had fallen in war were dealt with.* Still, this book mentions the role of Black men only once. After the fighting was over, it was apparently Black Americans who did most of the transport and reburial work. Their quartermaster remarked on this: "The treatment of the bodies was totally new for these Black men, but after they had seen how white personnel carried out the tasks, they proved quite efficient in the exercise of this gruesome task."

Until recently hardly anything could be found in Dutch

---

* Michael Sledge, *Soldier Dead: How We Recover, Identify, Bury and Honor our Military Fallen* (New York: Columbia University Press, 2017).

Arrival of new bodies (Source: SHOM)

archives or in historical books about the role of Black military workers. There are, however, a number of photos that show that Black Americans were the ones who carried out the grave digging.

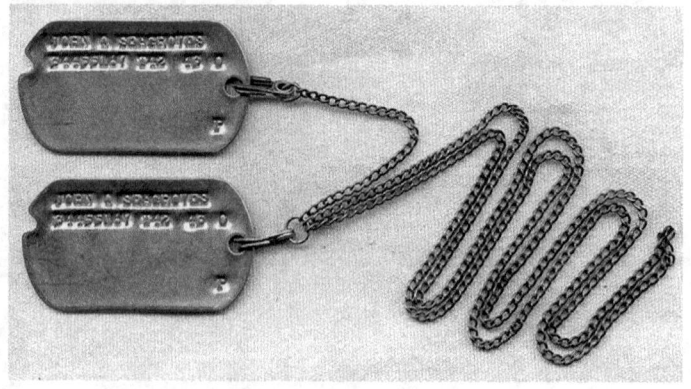

A part of the identity plate of a soldier (the so-called dog tag) was nailed to the temporary grave cross. The other part was placed in the mouth of the body before burial (Source: Wikipedia)

CHAPTER 4 – The Fields of Margraten

The day after arrival in Gronsveld on November 17, 1944, Jeff and the commanding officer of the GRC went to Margraten, to view the site where the cemetery work was to take place. He met Captain Shomon there for the first time, who was in charge of the construction of the cemetery.

Jeff: "We drove over muddy roads from Gronsveld to Margraten. It was cold and wet, halfway between rain and snow. The paths were hardly navigable. I noticed a tremendously awful smell, but I didn't realize at first that the stench came from a cemetery. On our way through France and Belgium we had smelled something similar, but not as bad as here. Upon arrival in Margraten, I saw fields lying full of bodies. Nothing but dead bodies. It shook me up tremendously.

A group of officers, inspectors, and volunteers stood around Captain Shomon, who supervised the whole operation. Shomon told us that we could start with the grave digging as soon as his soldiers had inspected the terrain. Further down there was a field with another four to five thousand dead soldiers, he said. That was on the site where the cemetery is nowadays. The dead bodies would be identified there. That had to take place before the burial would take place.

I was just nineteen then! And altogether upset. I felt totally nauseated by everything I saw there. The captain must have seen that, the way I looked. But he said nothing.

A bit later he took me aside, and I saw that he was trembling. He had known what we were assigned to do, he said, but had found it difficult to explain to the troops what they were in for. He was upset about the large number of dead soldiers that he saw that first day. I asked him what equipment was available other than the pickaxes and shovels that lay around. His answer was brief: 'You'll have to make do with this. Start with grave number one and continue down the row.'

The next morning the men of our company got onto army trucks and were taken to about a hundred yards from the entrance of the cemetery. Our first day as gravediggers was about to start. The captain, along with four other officers and four sergeants, stood waiting for us. The sergeants were to inspect whether the graves were dug in accordance with the rules and whether the dead were buried respectfully.

Captain Shomon said, 'Be aware that you are about to perform one of the most gruesome tasks possible. I don't envy you, but I don't feel sorry for you either. Because someone has to do it. Make sure that every grave is exactly six feet deep, six feet long, and two-and-a-half feet wide. And a chaplain will not always be available during the burial. Bury the dead with respect, even when it's hundreds per day. Remember that every soldier that you bury is an American. And that it could have been your own brother or cousin.'"

THE SOUND OF RAIN DROPS AND PICKAXES
Jeff: "What the men got to see was awful. I had wondered the night before what I should say to them. If I remember correctly – but my memory might fail me here – it was something like: 'This is one of the many tasks that need to get done in the army. And that task has landed on us. You're unhappy about it, and so am I, but it has to be done.' I added that they had to make sure to get a good pair of gloves, a sturdy shovel, and a pickaxe. One of the soldiers came up to me. His face was ashen. He asked, 'Sergeant, what happens if we do our best, but it turns out that we can't manage it? What can we then expect?' I answered, 'What happens then, I don't know, but I assume that each of you does what he can.'

The tarp cloths that the bodies were covered with were pulled away from the first row of dead soldiers. We saw more than two hundred bodies. As I now knew what our task was, I waited for large trucks laden with coffins. I thought that we couldn't start with burying without coffins. It took some time. I got impatient and asked a white sergeant when the coffins would arrive. He answered,

'There are no coffins.' Then he pointed to a pile of mattress covers and said, 'You'll get used to it. Just put the body in a cover, tie up the ends, and lower the body in the grave.'*

I was quite upset about the situation. The only dead person that I had ever seen in my life was my little sister. As poor as we were at the time, there was still a coffin. She was buried in it, in a new dress. But here, not a single coffin. Not even a box."

A DEAD SISTER

Jeff: "I had seen a dead person only once in my life. A sister of mine, eleven years old, got sick one day, and within two days she died. The nearest doctor lived eleven or twelve miles from us. My father tried to get him to come look at my sister. But at first he didn't want to come; I don't know whether that was because she was Black or because the distance was too great for him. When the doctor finally arrived, he took a look at her and said that she had a colic and that my parents needed to give her Castor oil, a really thick oil that caused diarrhea. My mother gave that to her, but the next day she was dead. Later we found out that she died because of appendicitis and that she should have had an operation. If that had happened in time, she would not have died."

---

* Mattress covers, made of sturdy smell- and mold-resistant cotton, so-called mattress ticking, were used for the first emergency funerals because of the shortage of coffins.

A body is placed in a mattress cover (Source: US Army Archives)

THE FIRST GRAVES

Jeff: "Somewhat later that first day a couple of huge army trucks rode up, filled with dead soldiers. They were piled up like tree trunks. When asked whether a few of our men would be willing to help unload, everyone ran toward the trucks. Anything was better than burying still more dead bodies, they apparently thought. Unloading seemed just a bit less gruesome than burying bodies. When you lowered someone into his grave, you were the last human being that the dead person had contact with.

Those days all you heard was the sound of rain drops and pickaxes. I don't remember anyone saying a word."*

---

* This refers to the bodily remains that were dug up again at emergency cemeteries or in mass graves. They were frozen during transport.

Wrapped in a mattress cover, a dead soldier is carried to his grave (Source: US Army Archives)

Jeff: "The first dead person that we buried was a German girl. I recall that part of her head had been shot away. She had been hit by a grenade, and her back revealed fifteen or more bullet holes. Before or after a grenade attack she must have also been shot numerous times with a machine gun. We took her from the American section of the cemetery to the enemy section.

German casualties were strictly separated from those of other nationalities. We had to see to it closely that not a single American soldier ended up in the enemy section, for even if that was accidental, you'd face a severe penalty.

Captain Shomon wasn't sure, but he and others speculated that the girl might have been a spy for the German army, reporting about enemy troop movements. What

Grave diggers of the 3138th QMSC in Margraten (Source: US Army Archives)

other reason could there have been to shoot down such a young girl? I never found out, but I still see her body in my mind's eye. We thought at the time that the war would soon end, certainly if the Germans were so desperate that they even involved women and children in the war effort.

But we were quite mistaken, as turned out later when we realized what was happening in Bastogne, in the Belgian Ardennes."

LONG DAYS

The 960th QMSC worked at the cemetery until December 18, 1944. Every single day the army trucks took the men of the unit from the school in Gronsveld to Margraten and back. In the spring of 1945, the unit returned briefly to Margraten.

Jeff: "Each day's ritual started with reveille. As soon as the bugle sounded, everyone stepped in line. One of my tasks was to ensure that everyone who had to be present was actually there. When the captain too was satisfied, then all two hundred and sixty of us could go to the breakfast area in the school building. Immediately after breakfast the trucks stood ready to drive us to Margraten.

In the days that followed, there were soldiers who simply couldn't stop working. When our lunch was brought at the cemetery, they kept on. I asked one of them once why he didn't pause. His answer: 'If I stop digging, I can't get started again.' Not a word of protest. These were youngsters who in their entire lives had never been confronted with anything as gruesome as this. Some of them cried during the work, especially when they lowered the mattress covers with bodies in it into the graves. They were totally upset.

Only shortly before, when we rode in trucks from Belgium towards Gronsveld, we talked a lot and told jokes. Also during meals the atmosphere was quite relaxed then. We would make up all sorts of stories, some of them quite exaggerated. But once we got to Margraten, the atmosphere changed. I can say, hand on my heart, that not a single joke was told during that whole time, and no laughing at all when approaching the cemetery or during the meals. The contrast was enormous. During meals the talking was confined to comments such as: 'Pass the mustard, or hand me a cup of coffee.' That was all. I believe we were all traumatized due to all the mutilations and wounds that we had seen."

LIVES TORN ASUNDER

Jeff: "Each day when we arrived in the morning we saw that a new supply of dead soldiers had been laid on the cold ground under a tar cloth. We'd pull the cloth away to see how many had to be buried that day. Sometimes there were hundreds of bodies waiting for us.*

---

* "Starting in November 1944, thousands of soldiers who were killed during the vehement battle for the Siegfried Line, the German city of Aachen, and Hürtgenwald, were brought to the American cemetery in Margraten. In the aftermath of the harsh Ardennes offensive, which had just been repelled, the enormous cemetery next to the highway from Maastricht to Vaals kept devouring terrible numbers of victims. [...] From the German hinterland [came] an endless column of 2.5-ton trucks and 1 trailers with the bodies of GIs who had been killed during Operation Grenade, the offensive to cross the Ruhr River. [The goal of Operation Grenade was for the American 9th Army, led by William Hood Simpson, to cross the Ruhr between Roermond and Düren in February 1945. It marked the start of the Allied invasion of Germany.] Operation Plunder was meant to push on across the Rhine. [...] Trucks continued to head for and return from Margraten. The number of killed soldiers who had to be buried each day was overwhelming, not just American but also German casualties. All of these bodies were buried first in the vicinity of the battlefields [in mass graves]. Right after the liberation of Southern Limburg, these bodies were brought to Margraten." (Peter Schrijvers, *De schaduw van de bevrijding, België 1944-1945*, 3rd ed. [Antwerp: Manteau, 2014], p. 286.)

'Just ten more, and then we're done for today,' we sometimes said to each other. But hardly had we said this when another truck arrived with anywhere from fifty to a hundred bodies. There was a permanent arrival of bodies, the whole day long. Sundays included, seven days a week.

I find it difficult, even now, to read in the paper that soldiers 'gave their lives.' I don't know if there is any soldier who truly 'gives' his life. All those boys in Margraten, their lives were taken away."

GIRLS FROM MARGRATEN

A group of girls, about ten years old, came looking nearly every day at the entrance of the cemetery, at some distance from us. At first, they stayed some fifty yards from the gravediggers. They stood there when Jeff and his men arrived. When the men left at the end of the day, they were there again. That went on for several weeks. Gradually the girls came closer.

Jeff: "Maybe the girls were a bit afraid because of stories that they had heard about us. Or they might never have seen Black people before. Yet I noticed that they gradually dared to get closer. Apparently, they had discovered that we were ordinary people, just like themselves. One of the girls, I guess she was about ten, ultimately dared to talk to me. She asked, 'Are you the boss?' I was surprised to hear that she spoke some English, and I responded by saying, 'Why do you think that?' She answered, 'Because you are the one talking the whole time.' Then she asked me things about back home. About America she didn't know much, but she had heard of New York. I told her that I did not come from New York. She also asked me where I would go when I left Margraten, what I would do at home. That was a unique encounter, there in Margraten, that I still remember well."

Elevated graves (Source: SHOM)

CHAPTER 5 – The Netherlands American Cemetery and Memorial

At that time, Margraten was the second largest American cemetery in Europe, next to that in Henri-Chapelle in Belgium. On March 30, 1946 the last body was buried in Margraten that came from one of the combat areas. American soldiers who had died were buried at random, regardless of rank, color, religion, or gender. Such is standard practice in American military cemeteries, ever since General J. J. Pershing led the US forces in Europe during World War I.

NUMBERS OF AMERICAN CASUALTIES BROUGHT TO MARGRATEN

Numbers based on a count in 1946:
- 17,738 Americans, of whom 955 unknown soldiers
- 3,075 Germans, of whom 2,776 unknown
- 1,026 allied soldiers, of whom 155 unknown
- 693 from the Soviet Union (probably also including forced laborers)

- plus 20 Italians, 8 Poles, 6 Czechoslovaks, 6 Greeks, 2 Rumanians, 2 Ukrainians, 2 Yugoslavs, and 1 Hungarian

In 1946 and 1947 the bodies of all German soldiers were exhumed by German prisoners of war and reburied in the Limburg village of Ysselsteyn.

War victims from the Soviet Union were transferred to the Soviet War Cemetery in Leusden (near Amersfoort) in 1948. The bodily remains of casualties from other nations were buried elsewhere, such as in Maastricht.*

DIVISION OF WORK

There was hardly any contact between Black and white American soldiers during the work at Margraten. And none at all after work. Did the inhabitants of Margraten notice any of this? One of them, Frans Douven, never forgot that when white soldiers entered his father's hotel, the Black soldiers who sat at the bar would abruptly end their conversation and submissively leave the building.

Jeff: "There were quite a few white American soldiers in Margraten, working together with us. Not as gravediggers, only we did that. But the truck drivers who brought the bodies from the battlefields to Margraten included both Blacks and whites. The men of the GRC, the graves registration unit, were white. They had the awful but key task of identifying each soldier before burial. So long as someone

---

* The burial of Black soldiers was not discussed during the interviews with Jeff in 2010.

The prefab wooden chapel, painted white with spray cans. It had a tower, constructed by prisoners of war from aluminum plates of planes that were shot down
(Source: SHOM)

had not been identified with certainty, the body would be laid aside until fingerprints and such had been collected. The GRC was very efficient. The more checks they carried out, the less chance of errors."

"My task was to carefully identify each body as American and to see to it that the gravediggers placed it respectfully in the grave. One day two soldiers were burying a body. I saw that they did not lower the body carefully but allowed it to fall. When I accosted them about this, they said it had happened by accident. That evening, after dinner, I got the whole company together to talk about what we encountered during the day. I used the opportunity to point out that the boys that we lowered in the ground had not asked to be killed. They deserved all the respect that we could give them."

GRUESOME, DIRTY WORK

Jeff: "It may sound bizarre, but we were glad that many of the soldiers that we had to bury in the beginning had only just been killed. Not more than two or three days before. But that quickly changed. The bodies of soldiers who had been killed more than a month ago were half decomposed. A special team helped us to place these bodies in mattress covers. I hope that no one will ever have to do this again. It sure wasn't a hygienic task, and we were never totally clean. The stench kept hanging around us when we got back in Gronsveld. It was gruesome, dirty work. At times there was hot water in the school, but if not, we then warmed water in our helmets, which we used as wash tubs. That's how we washed ourselves. After a few weeks shower wagons occasionally came to Margraten from an army depot in Maastricht, so we could shower once a week. I remember that one of those shower wagons stood right before the entrance of the cemetery. Each of us was expected to dig at least three graves a day. But we hardly managed that under those weather conditions. Margraten is the only place on earth that I ever was at, where it rained the whole time. At least that's how it felt. It was a mix of wind, rain, and snow. Cold, really cold! And the ground! The earth was sometimes frozen, or else completely soaked so that the clay stuck to your shovel. When you had dug a hole three feet deep, it could easily fill up again with mud and water before your very eyes. All so frustrating. Later I heard that the winter of 1944 was one of the coldest in Holland in years."

SOMETHING IS WRONG HERE!
Jeff: "So there we were. A group of Black Americans confronted with all these dead white Americans. I realized that we had to bury them, but when they were alive we couldn't sit in the same room. Something isn't right here, I thought. Our assignment was to lower them in the earth as respectfully as possible. Which we did. But that didn't mean that we'd forget the time before we ended up there in Margraten. At that time we didn't realize at all what impact Margraten would have on us for the rest of our lives, when back in our own country. What are you doing here, for God's sake? How did you end up here? I often asked myself this when seeing all those young faces, of Americans fallen in combat, all of them white. And I know for sure that I wasn't the only one who asked this. We must have buried some two hundred white boys a day on average. I purposely say 'boys' because some of them were probably hardly older than me, one of the youngest soldiers in the army. At the same time I realized that it had not been *my* intent to come here, but that I had been sent. And then I could only ask why. Why me? At a given moment I remembered a passage from the Bible: 'If the Lord had a certain task, everyone stood up and said: Here I am, Lord, let me do it.' But I had not asked the Lord to send me to Margraten. Absolutely not. Still there I was. And I saw all those young faces."

REFLECTING

Jeff: "Two years before arriving in Margraten I was nothing but a farm boy on a large plantation in Alabama. I couldn't get a decent education because the system didn't allow it. A decent job I didn't have either. Then suddenly I was in a country that I had never heard of, in a village called Margraten, in surroundings that in many respects looked like the farm land where I grew up. And I was tied down to a task that I wouldn't wish on anyone, that of gravedigger in a sprawling cemetery. Did I deserve this? I said to myself: don't get too melancholy, because you're not the only one in this plight. There are hundreds of others just like you. It is important that you ask yourself this type of question, but not here and now. I couldn't answer these questions in Margraten, or in Bastogne, or anywhere else in Europe. But they kept haunting me. During the day, but also at night.

Mrs. Merrill, who helped me in the library on Staten Island at the time, had often emphasized that after the war I should reflect on my status as a Black person: 'Not just you as a Black person, but we as a nation need to reflect on our status.' That helped me put my frustrations aside. I kept in mind that the war would be over one day. Then the time would be there to tackle this task. I think that it was not until the cold winter months of 1944 into 1945 that I fully realized what restrictions I had suffered back home as a Black person. And also that I needed to liberate myself from these, soon enough, in Alabama. How that would need to be done, I had no idea, but in any case it occupied me from that moment on."

THE FINAL DAY

Jeff: "We worked in Margraten until mid-December. We thought that the job of burying the dead was almost done. So we left Gronsveld and Margraten on December 18, 1944. What we didn't know then was that the Germans had forced a breakthrough during the Battle of the Bulge, leading to our brief return to Margraten in the spring of 1945.

The last time that we were brought to our quarters in the school in Gronsveld at the end of the working day, there was loud singing and praying in the trucks. It was a noisy ride. The soldiers thanked God that they wouldn't have to go back to Margraten, would no longer have to bury the dead. Some of them even cried, others started boozing it up. I had to ensure that nobody drank so much that it would be a risk to themselves or others. That sure wasn't easy. So difficult even that I even decided later in the evening to involve the MPs, the military police. I was afraid I wouldn't be able to handle the situation on my own. The MPs asked how many men had to be picked up. But I didn't want anyone to end up in prison. The MPs were quite resolute. They walked about, grabbed drunken soldiers by the collar if needed, and said to several of them, 'Get up and be gone. And sleep it off.'"*

---

* The 960th briefly returned to Margraten in the spring of 1945 to help out there.

REPATRIATION OF BODIES AND THE FORMALIZATION OF THE AMERICAN CEMETERY

A major repatriation of fallen soldiers took place in 1947. Prior to this, the US Army had asked relatives back home where they would want their family member to be buried, in Europe or in America. Nearly ten thousand corpses were repatriated, and on December 15, 1949 the cemetery was formally declared established. All fallen soldiers were reburied according to the definitive classification that we know now. Management of the cemetery was transferred that day from the US Army to the American Battle Monuments Commission, which falls under the US Department of Veteran Affairs. The official dedication took place on July 7, 1960, with Queen Juliana attending.

As of 2014 the Wall of the Missing lists 1,722 names. It has not been possible to identify all dead soldiers who are buried in Margraten. Their graves are marked by the words "Known Only to God.". The cemetery holds nearly 8,300 graves of identified fallen soldiers.

COMMEMORATION OF THE FALLEN, ADOPTION OF GRAVES

After the liberation of the Netherlands, the Limburg municipalities of Eijsden-Margraten and Maastricht received numerous letters from family members in search of the grave of their son, husband, or father. Else Hanöver, secretary to the Maastricht mayor Willem Michiels van Kessenich at the time, assisted in answering these letters, which were generally received via the Red Cross. She also established contacts between relatives and people living near the cemetery. That was the start of the Foundation for Adopting Graves of Margraten. All graves and the names of missing soldiers were adopted by local residents, already since Memorial Day in May 1946. Every grave continues to be adopted, sometimes by the fourth generation of one and the same family.

In 2015 the Faces of Margraten Foundation was founded, and 3,300 photos were placed next to the graves during a special ceremony. The Fields of Honor Database meanwhile contains more than 7,000 photos.

RACE CODE 2: THE 172 AFRICAN AMERICANS OF MARGRATEN

The Margraten cemetery also includes the graves of African American soldiers who died during World War II, and the Wall of the Missing contains the names of missing African Americans. I was unaware of this until 2014, as were those who adopted the graves and names of missing soldiers. In the fall of that year I received a list containing the names of the African American dead soldiers buried in Margraten and of those missing from Keith Stadler, superintendent of the American cemetery at the time.

Not until then had anyone heard that Black Americans (other than Willy F. James Jr.) were buried in Margraten. The list was compiled on the basis of the original burial certificates. These include categories such as name, grave, number, and religion, but also race. Race code 2 stands for Black American casualties. Race code 1 for white Americans.

Further research provided evidence that there were 172 Black Americans in Margraten cemetery. Thirty-two of them belonged to the 2,221 Negro Infantry Volunteers, who had reported following a call by General Lee (see Chapter 6, Exceptions).

Meanwhile, with the assistance of the Dutch embassy in Washington, DC, research is being conducted to answer the question, "Who were these 172 African American soldiers who left for Europe?"

DECORATION FOR THE 960TH QUARTERMASTER COMPANY

In a letter dated March 4, 1945, Captain Shomon commended the 960th QMSC for the outstanding work that it had performed at Margraten. His words of praise did not, however, reach the members of that company at the time. It was not until 2007 that Captain Keith Archibald of the former 960th Quarter Master Company (US Army Reserves) discovered the report about the unit. Along with the report, he found the decoration* in the archives of the Ninth Army in the US Army Center of Military History.**

Archibald then succeeded in tracing three veterans of the unit, Albert Smaha, William Solms, and Jefferson Wiggins. He invited them to a meeting during which the Meritorious Unit Commendation streamer was attached to the banner of the unit.

---

* The decoration the unit didn't received than, but Jefferson Wiggins, First Sergeant of the 960th QMSC belatedly received the decoration in 2007.
** US Army Center of Military History.

Drawn portrait of Willy F. James Jr. (Source: National World War II Museum in New Orleans)

Grave of Willy F. James Jr. (Photo: Mieke Kirkels)

Burial certificate with race code 2 (Source: American Battle Monuments Commission)

Letter by President Obama (Source: Wiggins collection)

CHAPTER 6 – American Policy against Racism in Wartime

"The world's greatest democracy fought the world's greatest racist with a segregated army."
– Stephen E. Ambrose

In his State of the Union Address on January 6, 1941, President Franklin D. Roosevelt called the United States the "arsenal of democracy" and presented the "four freedoms": the freedom of speech, the freedom of worship, the freedom from want, and the freedom from fear.* "Americanism," according to Roosevelt, "is a matter of mind and heart and is not and never was a matter of race or ancestry."

African Americans clearly saw the hypocrisy between their conditions at home and the noble goals set by their president for World War II. An enormous gap existed between promises and greater freedom for Blacks and the everyday practice in terms of racial relations. Few African Americans felt motivated to get involved in the war effort and to work in the war industry. The Black labor union leader A. Philip Randolph threatened in 1941 to call for a

---
* See www.fourfreedoms.nl

massive march on Washington.* This threat convinced Roosevelt that the discrimination of African Americans in the weapons industry needed to end. That was just the beginning.

The confrontation with the Aryan racist policy of the Nazi regime compelled the US to reconsider its own policy regarding the multicultural society.

THE DOUBLE V CAMPAIGN

"We cannot condemn Nazism, with its Aryan overtures, when we don't have our own affairs in order."

With more than a million Black Americans participating in World War II, self-awareness grew fast among the Black communities in the United States. The public media in the United States, in particular the Black media, faced a dilemma during the war. Should they adhere, without batting an eyelid, to government propaganda that spoke of tremendous harmony between Blacks and whites in the US and its army – propaganda that was regarded as necessary because of the war and that was meant to demonstrate national unity? Or should they tell the truth? In the latter case they would be seen as enemies of the state. How should Black media, journalists, and spokesmen present themselves?

---

* Philip Randolph (1889–1979) was a labor union official and politician and one of the many leaders of the civil rights movement. He took the initiative for the Brotherhood of Sleeping Car Porters, the first union that consisted mainly of African Americans. During World War II he led the March on Washington movement. (Source: "A. Philip Randolph." *History*, October 27, 2009, https://www.history.com/topics/black-history/a-philip-randolph.).

A leading Black newspaper, *The Pittsburgh Courier*, came up with a solution that considered both sides of the matter. It launched the Double V Campaign, which stood for Victory Abroad and Victory at Home. African Americans were encouraged to dedicate themselves fully to the war effort. At the same time, the government was called upon to do everything possible to live up to the Declaration of Independence and to realize equal treatment for every citizen, regardless of race.* The campaign fiercely condemned racism in the world's greatest democracy; it was a prelude to the post-war civil rights movement.

EXCEPTIONS

Pressured by the NAACP, the National Association for the Advancement of Colored People, President Roosevelt tried to raise the recruitment of African Americans for the army so that their level of participation in the army would correspond with their share in the population, 10.6 percent. Although the number of Black soldiers did increase, this percentage was never achieved.

Of the 1.2 million Black Americans who served in Europe, 780 died in action. Others died of illness or traffic accidents. Only late in the war did they get sufficient training to be sent to Europe.**

---

* The Declaration of Independence was written by Thomas Jefferson and adopted on July 4, 1776.
** "Of the 1,200,000 black soldiers who served during World War II, 780 lost their lives in fighting. In addition, many died of illnesses or due to accidents while serving in the army. Only a small number of them received thorough training before departure for Europe, although this

Others, too, called upon the government to get itself in proper order so that it could unashamedly confront the Nazis when condemning the German Aryan race doctrine. A Republican politician said about this: "We cannot suffice with combatting imperialism overseas while maintaining a form of imperialism at home."* Especially Lieutenant-General Leslie McNair and the president's wife, Eleanor Roosevelt, advocated the abolition of racial segregation in the army. This led to the establishment by the War Department of a commission that was charged with promoting integration in the armed forces.

The 761st tank battalion, established on March 15, 1942 in Camp Claiborne, Louisiana, was one of the first fully Black combat units. The 784th tank battalion, which was involved in the liberation of the Dutch city of Venlo, also consisted entirely of Black soldiers. Similar units included the Tuskegee Airmen** and the 320th Barrage Balloon Com-

---

situation improved some as the war effort progressed. President Roosevelt's priority was victory in war. It was his wife Eleanor who took steps during the war to improve the position of blacks, and it was President Truman who ultimately abolished segregation in the US army." (Source: Prof. Bob Solomon, Penn State University)

* Roosevelt.

** The Tuskegee Airmen were the first African American aviators in the segregated US armed forces during World War II, but they were seriously discriminated against both in the army and in daily life. They trained at the military airfield in Tuskegee, Alabama. They never took part in the fighting. Instead, their duties included accompanying bombers. (Source: "Who Are the Tuskegee Airmen of World War II," Tuskegee Airmen National Historical Museum, https://tuskegeemuseum.org/history/#:~:text=Who%20are%20the%20Tuskegee%20Airmen,skill%2C%20courage%2C%20and%20patriotism).

Soldiers of the 761st All Black Tank Battalion in Venlo in 1945 (Source: US Army Archives)

pany. Plus, there were the 2,221 Negro Infantry Volunteers to replace white infantries killed in Normandy and the Battle of the Bulge.*

TEMPORARY DESEGREGATION, BORN OUT OF NEED
In December 1944, the infantry divisions of the American army in Europe, which consisted entirely of white sol-

---

* This was the only African American fighting unit at D-Day. Even though stories about D-Day seldom mentioned Black soldiers, two thousand of them nonetheless were involved in combat situations. These included the 621 members of the 320th Barrage Balloon Battalion, infantrymen who tried to hinder German planes that were underway to the Normandy coast with special large balloons (Hervieux, *Forgotten*).

diers, experienced a great shortage. This was due to the high number of infantrymen who were killed in action, especially during the Battle of the Bulge. In light of this, Lieutenant-General John C. H. Lee recommended to Commander-in-Chief Dwight Eisenhower to call upon African American soldiers stationed in Europe to join the infantry on a voluntary basis. Eisenhower was inclined to do so, but he realized all too well that racial integration in the army and in American society as a whole was still a sensitive subject. He therefore urged Lee to recruit both Black and white volunteers. The call, which took place on December 26, 1944, led to some five thousand African American soldiers responding within two months. The number was so high that their superiors feared that they would no longer be able to perform their tasks adequately. Hardly any white volunteers reported. About half of the Black volunteers started infantry training in Compiègne in France. However, they had to give up their rank, to prevent them from being placed above whites in terms of rank. Ultimately 2,221 were trained for their new position. In March 1945 they were added to white divisions as separate platoons. In that way a temporary desegregation was achieved.

Not a single one of these 2,221 soldiers got official recognition after the war for their share in the infantry, not even posthumously. This error was only adjusted much later, under pressure. After thorough research, 743 reports were located about these men. Of these, forty-six ultimately received the Bronze Star, mostly posthumously. The rank that they fulfilled before they voluntarily entered the infantry was also returned to them.*

THE ONLY COLORED R&R CENTER

The Rest and Recreation (R&R) Center for Blacks Only established in the Belgian town of Eisden was quite exceptional. All R&R centers of the American army during World War II were for whites only, while the catering services were generally provided by Black Americans of a QMSC.

Because of the special contribution of Black Americans during the Battle of the Bulge, the leadership of the 9th Army decided to set up a Colored R&R for the 7th Armored Division in Eijsden, in the Netherlands. By mistake this came to be situated in the Belgian town of Eisden, on the other side of the Meuse River. Former colonel Max R. Wise wrote in a 1995 letter to the mayor of Eijsden, that, as army major at the time, he had been in charge of the establishment of R&Rs. He wrote: "The only R&R for colored troops in the history of the US was set up in the Dutch province of Limburg..." Only later did he get word, from heritage expert Jan Kohlbacher from Maasmechelen in Belgium, that this special R&R had in fact been set up in Eisden in Belgium.

---

* Records Concerning the Association of the 2,221 Negro Volunteers (World War II Soldiers). Clinton Presidential Library.

The only black R&R in the history of the US army, erroneously established in the Belgian town of Eisden instead of the Dutch town of Eijsden (Source: Jan Kohlbacher and letters of Max Wise)

ABOLITION OF RACIAL SEGREGATION IN THE US ARMY
In 1947 A. Phillip Randolph, together with his colleague Grant Reynolds, made a new attempt to bring an end to segregation in the US Army. They founded the Committee Against Jim Crow in Military Service and Training. The name was later changed to League for Non-Violent Civil Disobedience Against Military Segregation.

With Executive Order 8802, issued on June 25, 1941, President Roosevelt had banned discriminatory employment practices by federal agencies and all unions and companies engaged in war-related work.* This meant equal treatment and opportunity for US citizens, regardless of race, religion, or national origin. But the activists were not yet satisfied and exerted further pressure. Because of the special contributions made by African American units during World War II, President Truman ordered the total abolition of racial segregation in the US armed forces with Executive Order 9981, which was enacted on July 26, 1948.

Although it would still take years before desegregation within all sections of the armed forces was a fact, discrimination on the basis of race now formally belonged to the past.

---

* In a statement issued on July 26, 1918, President Woodrow Wilson wrote, "There have been many lynchings, and every one of them has been a blow at the heart of ordered law and humane justice. No man who loves America, no man who really cares for her fame and honor and character, or who is truly loyal to her institutions, can justify mob action while the courts of justice are open and the governments of the States and the Nation are ready and able to their duty" (Woodrow Wilson, "My Fellow Countrymen ..." July 26, 1918. Library of Congress Printed Ephemera Collection; portfolio 241, folder 18).

CHAPTER 7 – Professional Soldier or Civilian?

A troop ship carried Jeff back to the United States in seven days. While on board an important question occupied him, which he quickly had to find an answer to after homecoming: will I become a professional soldier or lead a civilian life? He roughly knew what to expect of a life as a professional soldier. But what life as a civilian would entail, that he had no idea of. In the army he knew that he was respected for who he was, for his qualities and dedication. He wondered whether that would also apply to a life outside the military. If he wanted to build a civilian life, he would have to go to school and learn a profession or a trade. The study guide of the university that he had gotten showed that he would have to start by getting a high school diploma. But he had no idea how. After all, he had not even finished grade school. And would he be admitted to a high school?

The army gave him sixty days to make up his mind.

Jeff: "Once I arrived in New York, everything went smooth at first. You could take the subway and go wherever you wanted. After a couple of weeks, I took leave to go to Alabama to visit my family. But as soon as I got underway, the shit started again, right after leaving Washington, DC. There I sat on the train, an army officer, someone who had helped bury nearly twenty thousand soldiers. In the train there were signs that said that the front part, the dirtiest part full of soot, was for Blacks. The cleaner part in the back was for 'Whites Only.' I had to change cars, dammit! How did I deserve this? What would all those dead soldiers that we had buried think of this if they could talk? I was totally upset, furious too.

In Fort Rucker, not far from Dothan, my home town, it was even worse. German prisoners of war were housed there under far more luxurious circumstances than most of us. They had better food, recreational facilities, and healthcare, and access to better education than our kids. Our kids could only hope to learn anything at the segregated schools, which were absolutely inferior. The prisoners of war could move about freely within the county limits. They sat in the front of the bus, while we, Black Americans, had to sit in the back. There were quite a few stores with 'Whites Only' signs on the door. The Germans could go in, but not me!

The war brought us, Black Americans, not a single sign of appreciation or praise. The situation back then, as I look at it now, was pretty explosive, so explosive that changes were bound to come. What's more, they were absolutely necessary."

ALL MEN ARE CREATED EQUAL

Jeff: "After a week or two at home, I went back to New York. The first thing I did was look up Mrs. Merrill again. She obviously wanted to know all about my experiences as a liberator in Europe. After I had told her all the details, she asked me what my plans were. I didn't have any. I needed her advice and asked her. What is my assignment, my task? Her answer was simple, but difficult to fulfill: 'The only person who can tell you that is you yourself.' Yes, I sighed, I know. Next she quoted a couple of sentences by President Jefferson: 'All men are created equal. They are endowed by their Creator with certain unalienable rights.' She told me to think seriously whether I believed that, whether that could help in finding an answer to the question regarding my goal in life. She kept hammering that I should understand well that nothing would change for anyone so long as you didn't exert yourself.

This must have applied for many Black men who returned from Europe. It turned out that during World War II a movement had already come about for equal rights for Black people. But that was not yet an organized civil rights movement. Many priests and ministers spoke in the churches about civil rights, all right. And people in Black community organizations talked about it, but that did not constitute an organized movement."

WHO WERE THE HEROES?

Most books, movies, and documentaries about World War II give the impression that the heroes and liberators were white soldiers, that it was only white men who demonstrated courage and made sacrifices during the war. For example, the movie *Saving Private Ryan*, viewed by millions, did not show a single African American in the scenes regarding D-Day.

It has gradually become clear that this picture is hardly correct. Even if African Americans were mainly charged with support services such as provisioning, maintenance, and transport during World War II, their work behind the frontlines was of vital importance to the war effort. And African Americans were definitely involved in combat situations, even if on an exceptional basis.

Black troops provided support to the combatants, from the beaches of Normandy to the heartland of Germany. And 2,221 *Negro Infantry Volunteers* participated in the fighting during the final two months of the war.

Of the 1.2 million African American soldiers who served during World War II, 780 died in combat. Many others died from illnesses or accidents in wartime. Only few got thorough training before leaving for Europe, although that situation improved later on during the war.

One of the American organizations that is active in changing the general perception regarding the participation of Black Americans in World War II is the Association of the 2,221 Negro Volunteers.

In the Netherlands, one of the museums displaying information regarding the role of African Americans in the nation's liberation is the Freedom Museum in Groesbeek (near Nijmegen).

PASTOR BROWN

Pastor Matthew Southall Brown Sr., one of the 2,221 Negro Infantry Volunteers, visited the Netherlands in September 2019. His visit, like that by Jefferson Wiggins ten years earlier, has been key to the Dutch perception of the role of Black American liberators. Pastor Brown personally initiated this visit. In 2016 I had interviewed him by telephone and email regarding "the 2,221." In May 2019 he informed me that he intended to come to the Netherlands, in particular to visit the cemetery in Margraten. After I notified the American embassy in The Hague of his planned visit, the embassy passed this information to the National Committee, which coordinates the annual commemorations of

Pastor Matthew Brown in Terneuzen in 2019, representing the United States Embassy of the Netherlands in Washington, DC, February 13, 2020 (Source: M. Beekman)

the Dutch liberation from Nazi Germany on May 4 and 5. This committee looked for seven veterans, one from each of the former allied nations, for the official start of "75 Years of Freedom," that year's commemoration in Terneuzen in September 2019. It was wonderful to see this Black American veteran sitting in the first of the seven jeeps that drove past the platform, and shaking hands with the Dutch and Belgian royal couples who attended this celebration. Back in the States, Brown said, "I shook hands with royals! I feel like a king!"

After Terneuzen, Pastor Brown visited the American cemetery in Margraten, where thirty-two of the 2,221 Negro Infantry Volunteers are buried. One of them, Julius A. Lawrence, became a friend of Matthew Brown during their military stay in Germany.

Pastor Brown was honored for his involvement at the Civil Rights Movement several times. Among others: In 2017 he received the Certificate Silver Life Membership from the NAACP (National Association for the Advancement of Colored People). In 2019 - at the annual Dr. Martin Luther King Jr. gala event - he was honored as the Preachers Pastor, for his continuing efforts on behalf of society, both as veteran and visionary.

Pastor Matthew Southall Brown Sr. died on November 21, 2021 in Savannah, Georgia at the age of 99.

BELIEVE IN YOURSELF

In the late 1940s, fears and threats continued to dominate the lives of African Americans. There was one thing, however, that the ruling elite in the South realized all too well: the US Constitution says that it is the people who decide who governs. The only way in which the Southern elite could govern was by winning elections. That led to well-organized attempts to prevent African Americans from exercising the right to vote. Such initiatives also took place in Houston County in Alabama, where Jeff lived.

Jeff: "We were quite aware that it was altogether necessary that we accepted that we were Americans. We had to believe in that. We would have to act as such if we found that we had the same rights as white Americans. We also knew that we had to develop a proper strategy. I was not quite happy at the time that some Black leaders called for violent protest. The people that I was in touch with did not want violence. Many of us had seen too many dead Americans, and too many dead Germans, Canadians, British. More violence would lead to more Margraten and more Normandy. We believed that the way of violence was not right.

Mrs. Merrill once said to me, 'Around the year 1600 the first Blacks were brought here from Africa. From that time on, we white people decided who and what you are and what you must think. That has to change, but I cannot change it for you. I can also not tell you how you should do that. All I know is that it must happen.' That way I slowly drew a picture of the direction I had to go, and it gradually became clear what I wanted to do with my life."

THE CIVIL RIGHTS MOVEMENT

The year 1909 saw the founding of the first organization that formally strove for full civil rights for African Americans: the NAACP, the National Association for the Advancement of Colored People. Woodrow Wilson, who was president of the US from 1912 to 1921, originally maintained racial segregation in government institutions, arguing that, even though he was against it, he could not act differently because of social tensions. During his re-election campaign in 1916 he was attacked by the NAACP because of his policy on race. In 1918, however, the NAACP achieved its first major success, as President Wilson issued a prohibition against lynching. In a speech that he held on July 26, 1918 he condemned the many lynchings that took place at the time.

The participation of African American soldiers in World War I, and especially their stay in Europe, led to an increased feeling of self-esteem among the Black population. In Europe they had regular contact with white people, something that was altogether new for them. That gradually led to changes, but also to counteraction on the part of white Americans. An often heard saying in the 1930s was: "They [Black veterans] were spoiled by French women."

The start of the segregation of the US Army was in 1942 and lasts till 1948, that is, including the entire period of its involvement in World War II. On January 10, 1957, during his State of the Union address, President Eisenhower said: "Steadily we are moving closer to the goal of fair and equal treatment of citizens without regard to race or color. But unhappily much remains to be done."

When John F. Kennedy became president in 1960, interest in the civil rights of Black Americans grew again. However, a long list of domestic and international issues caused them to remain low on the priority list of his administration. President Kennedy did improve the situation of Black Americans through small gestures that would not cause much commotion. He initiated the Commission on Equal Employment Opportunity, which led to better job opportunities for African Americans to some extent. And he called for legislation that was enacted after his death by his successor as president, Lyndon B. Johnson.

In 1965, a series of protest marches was held from Selma, Alabama, to the state capitol in Montgomery. These marches were organized by nonviolent activists to protest against African American citizens being prevented from exercising their voting rights. Abject violence was used by state troopers. President Johnson and the US Congress decided to show determination and defend the voting right of African Americans. This led to the signing on August 6, 1965 of the Voting Rights Act. It thereby became illegal to require reading ability tests for voters. Sharp supervision was initiated at voting sites. With this legislation, discrimination of African Americans and of women became punishable, like discrimination fraud during elections. However, exclusion of African Americans from elections did not fully end. Election fraud continued to take place for many years in a number of states. In 1970 and again in 1975, Congress expanded the Voting Rights Act.

LIFE AS A CIVILIAN

After much deliberation, Jeff decided to leave the army and go to school. He obtained a high school diploma on the basis of his merits in Europe. He owed this especially to the efforts of Mrs. Merrill. She had drawn up a petition and sent this to the Board of Education in Jeff's hometown. This petition mentioned, among other things, that Jeff had made it to the position of officer during his time in the army.

Jeff: "It was fantastic to get this diploma, even though not everyone on the education board was happy about it. When I was interviewed by the board, one of the members addressed me as 'boy.' Luckily, the other board members protested right away. After also being granted a scholarship, I could apply for college. I decided to study history and political science at Tennessee State University in Nashville. After graduating in 1949, I went to Houston County in Alabama. There I tried to get a teaching job at one of county schools. But I wasn't accepted anywhere. Maybe the school boards had a preconceived notion that this young Black man, recently back from Europe and with a few years of college behind him, would not be easy to handle."

TEACHER AND PEACE ACTIVIST

Jeff: "Instead of a teaching job at a county school, I found work at the Department of Veteran Affairs. The department had founded a high school for dropouts. All Black veterans who had not completed their high school education – that was the majority – were eligible for this supplementary schooling. Outside class hours I was a member of an action group for voting rights. We knew all too well that we couldn't achieve anything without the right to vote. Twice a week we went to the county courthouse and tried to register as voters. Time and again we were rejected, but every Tuesday and Friday we were back. We kept getting turned away, and often we were arrested for causing civil unrest. But we kept this up for quite some time."

ANOTHER WAR

In 1950 Jeff was called up for the Pacific War, in Korea. His position was altered from inactive to active reserve officer, and not long afterwards he left for South Korea, serving there as first lieutenant. Officially there were no segregated army units anymore, but that did not mean that racial segregation belonged to the past entirely. For example, there were still very few African American officers.*

Jeff spoke little, however, about his time in Korea. His wife Janice later told me: "World War II left a much greater

---

* Jeff explicitly called it a war. The United States provided the majority of the United Nations troops that supported South Korea in expelling the North Koreans and then protected the border between the two Koreas. ("Korean War," *History*, May 11, 2022, https://www.history.com/topics/asian-history/korean-war)

Painted portrait of Jeff Wiggins, by a Korean painter, name unknown. Made during Jeff's time in Korea around 1950 (Photo: Janice Wiggins Family)

impression on him than Korea. Europe had much more impact on him in his early years, but now he was older. During World War II he was an officer in a segregated army. Now he was an officer in a quite recently integrated army and had to lead white soldiers. Even though there were many more white than Black officers, the army was now no longer segregated. Personally, he had never been close to an African American officer prior to that, so he had no role model. That made it a totally different experience."

After a Black boy was shot dead in the street, President Harry S. Truman announced the end of racial segregation in the US armed forces. On July 26, 1948 he signed an executive order to that effect (Source: Chicago Defender, national edition, July 26, 1948)

NO QUICK CHANGES

After his return from Korea, Jeff stayed once with his mother in Alabama. On a Sunday morning, he had to get up at five o'clock. His mother had asked him the night before to drive her to a church in Montgomery, the capital of the state.

Jeff: "She wanted to go and listen to a new minister. I had my doubts whether it would be worth driving all the way there, no less than ninety miles, but my mother insisted. She definitely wanted to go there, and I had to bring her. I was not much impressed by what she told me about this minister. I had heard good sermons before. Except for the few people who had urged my mother to go listen to this young man, no one in my surroundings knew him. The name of this minister was Martin Luther King Jr.

The church where the sermon was to take place was not very big; it could hold about three hundred people. Upon arrival we saw immediately that the building was totally crowded. There was no air conditioning in those days, so all church windows were open. People who had not managed to get a place inside could follow the sermon outside. We sat down and waited for Dr. King.

When the choir lowered its volume, Dr. King entered the church. He seemed like an ordinary man, no one special. A bit short, with a potbelly. Well, I thought, so that's him, the man for whom I had to drive all this way. I wonder what he has to say. The choir sang, 'Mine eyes have seen the glory of the coming of the Lord.'

Then Dr. King walked towards the altar. He said that we had listened to one of his favorite songs. When he began to speak, the image I had of him changed all at once. He immediately and quite directly faced the veterans who were in the church, the men who had just returned from the war. He knew that they were inclined to be short-tempered. They had seen so many people fall in action, seen so many people die. He understood what we had had to endure and what newly gained insights we had brought with us from the war. He emphasized in his sermon that democracy is far superior to fascism and that any nation

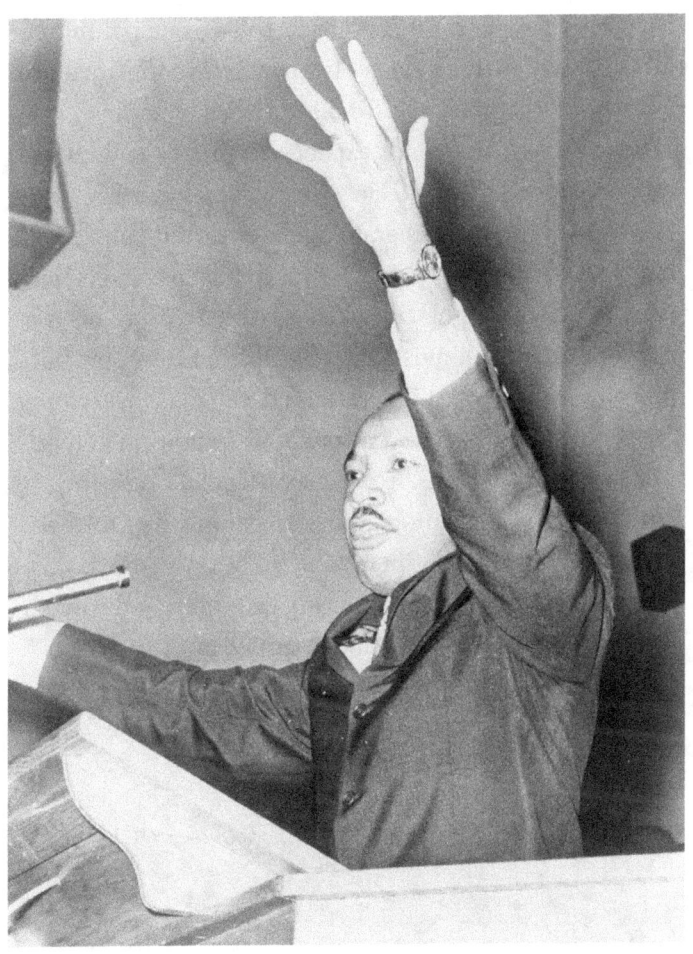

Martin Luther King, Jr. (Source: Wikimedia Commons)

that keeps people from exercising their principal human rights is on the wrong side of history. Everybody obviously understood this message. To all the Black veterans in the audience he said, 'Do not expect that things will change from one day to the next.' He gave examples of other countries that had tried to liberate themselves and pointed out that it takes time to achieve great changes. 'Everything happens at the right time.' Those words from his sermon impressed me most. He quoted from the Bible book of Ecclesiastes: 'There is a time and place for everything. There is a time to kill and a time to refrain from killing, a time for joy and a time for sorrow.' He ended his sermon by saying: 'Now is the time for your freedom. The future will not be easy, and it will not come all at once. Maybe that freedom will not even come during your lives, or during my own life. But it will come.' And he turned out to be right.

CHAPTER 8 – A Long Career in Education

After his service during the Korean conflict, Jeff decided to go and live in Newark, New Jersey. What was there to keep him in Alabama? He saw no opportunities, no future for himself there. He also decided to follow a program in educational studies and registered at Trenton State College in New Jersey.

But even with a university education, he found it difficult to find a job. In the early 1960s he worked in all sorts of jobs. He did factory work, was a handyman, worked as chauffeur in a parking lot. For lots of jobs it was decided that his educational level was too high. In the end, he got an office job at a bank, so that he finally earned a somewhat acceptable salary. But banking work quickly bored him, just like the job that he got next, as logistics staffer in a manufacturing company.

Finally, however, he found a job that was a perfect match for him and that he was altogether happy with, despite the lower salary. He became education director at a Children and Service Organization, a non-profit entity that provided reading and math courses to elementary and high school level students. That meant the start of an educational career that lasted over thirty years, until his retirement. After retiring he continued to teach, but as a volunteer.

Jeff met his wife Janice when working at Upsala College in New Jersey as director of the College Community Program, a program with which the university sought to stimulate more engagement in living with Black students and communities and with social issues. In 1996 Jeff and Janice moved to New Fairfield in Connecticut, where Jeff worked as a teacher, mentor, and speaker. He was a regular speaker on the topic of the multicultural society. He was firmly convinced that better cooperation between the various races and religions would lead to a better society. Together with his wife he founded the Wiggins Institute of Social Integrity in 2001.

In 1999 Jeff Wiggins received an honorary doctorate in Humane Letters at Briarwood College in Southington, Connecticut. Two years later he was decorated as Connecticut Multicultural Educator of the Year. In December 2005, Governor M. Jodi Rell declared a Jefferson Wiggins Day in the state of Connecticut.

CHAPTER 9 – Lessons of Margraten

Jeff: "After we left Margraten, the men of our company hardly had the chance to talk about what we had experienced, or about how we felt. We were so uncertain! When looking back after sixty-five years to that time in Margraten, I see various lessons to learn from.
- War means death.
- The more death, the more sorrow.
- The more sorrow, the more frustration.

We must learn to solve our disputes without killing each other. I mourn the American soldiers who died in that war, all the allied soldiers who were killed. But I also mourn the Germans who died.

We must not be afraid to talk with each other. There is no reason to end conflicts with bombs, gun fire, mortar shells. Enter negotiations instead. We must sit down at the negotiation table and do our damned best to solve disputes. We called the Germans our enemies, and that is what the Germans called us. If there are enemies on both sides, then we should be prepared to resolve differences, to say to each other: maybe it is not necessary to be each other's enemy. Look at what is happening, let's talk about that.

That's the kind of thing that went through my head and still occupies my mind.

A war can open your eyes. The Second World War ultimately had major effects for Black Americans. We didn't realize it then, but the war did bring us quite some benefits. When I was in the Netherlands in 2009, I spoke with various journalists and emphasized that the civil rights movement actually had its origins in the Second World War. During that war white and Black became more and more equal. Those journalists and also others that I met during my stay in Margraten had in fact never heard of the racial segregation in the US Army that helped liberate the Netherlands.

The dedication and motivation of Americans that led to the end of the war was more or less the same for everyone, white or Black. Following the war, when we Black Americans were back home again, we could no longer accept the conditions in our own country. We no longer accepted being treated as if we were lesser humans. I believe that every Black American who experienced the war in Europe was adamant about effecting change after returning home.

My country at least had to find a new way of dealing with us. The subject of civil rights was not talked about much during the war. But we undoubtedly realized this: if

Jeff Wiggins and Fritz Laab shaking hands. Laab worked on the construction of an emergency chapel at Margraten cemetery as a German prisoner of war in 1946
(Photo: Jody Gemmell)

we were good enough as a group to be sent to France, Belgium, the Netherlands, and other countries to liberate the people there, then we ought to be able to liberate ourselves in America also. Upon my return to the US after World War II, I wasn't sure what to expect, but I felt that things were about to change. Later on I found out that both Jeff and Fritz Laab had been at the Normandy beaches."

CHAPTER 10 – Back to Margraten: A Telephone Call from the Past

Stichting Akkers van Margraten (Fields of Margraten Foundation) was founded in 2008 by the Samenwerkende Heemkunde Organisaties Margraten (Joint Margraten Local History Organizations), as part of a Dutch national project called "Heritage of World War II – Eyewitness Stories." This was with a view to the sixty-fifth anniversary, in 2009, of the liberation of the province of Limburg from German occupation. The focus of the project was on the following question: *What was the impact on the farmers of Margraten when they had to accept, without previous warning, that thousands of bodies were dropped in their fertile fields?* The intent was to collect the recollections of the farmers and local residents in a book and a documentary. The film makers who were approached for this, Eugenie Jansen and Albert Elings, recorded all interviews on film.

One of the first people that I interviewed said that she had felt great compassion "with those black boys." I had no

← Jeff and Janice (May 2008) visiting the house of
F.D. Roosevelt (Photographer unknown)

idea what she was talking about. I am a baby boomer, born in 1947 and had never heard of Black American soldiers being involved in the war. It turned out that I was not the only one. History books never mentioned anything about them, and not even NIOD, the Dutch Institute for War Documentation, had information on them in its archives.

Late in 2008 the film makers traveled to the US to interview some of the white American veterans who had helped at the time with the construction of the American cemetery. They had the clear assignment to search American archives for former gravediggers and to interview them.*

In January 2009 they returned with some good interviews, but they had been unable to find anything in US archives about gravediggers. Without at least one interview with one of the hundreds of gravediggers, the story was not complete as far as I was concerned. But what could be done about it? The editing of the documentary and the book had to get started, because they had to be presented in September.

UNEXPECTED CONTACT WITH A GRAVEDIGGER
Then two weeks later, I happened to get a message, via the website www.akkersvanmargraten.nl, from a woman in Georgia named Sherry Barbour. She wrote that the website was particularly relevant for her neighbor, former Captain

---

* Eugenie Jansen and Albert Elings produced the documentary *Akkers van Margraten* (2009), which showed eyewitness stories in the Netherlands and the US about the construction of the American cemetery in Margraten.

William Solms, whom she knew to have supervised gravediggers in Margraten at the time. I knew by then that Black and white American soldiers had returned to the US separately and that most veteran organizations at the time were for whites only. The chance that Solms would still be in contact with Black gravediggers was small.

Mrs. Barbour provided me with Solms' telephone number, and I called him, hoping that he might have names and other information regarding former gravediggers. Solms told me that he had run into one of the gravediggers by chance two years earlier, in 2007, for the first time since World War II, during a military ceremony. His name was Jefferson Wiggins. And they had exchanged telephone numbers.

The first time I called Jeff Wiggins, in January 2009, his wife Janice answered the phone. She said, "I'll give you Jeff," and I heard him talk to her: "Someone from the Netherlands wants to know something about Margraten."

Jeff told me later that he had felt his blood pressure go up. He had never wanted to think about Margraten ever again. The only time the name of the village had come back to him was in 2007. Along with two other veterans of the 960th company – both of them white – he had been invited to receive an award for their unit. The name Margraten was mentioned, but after the ceremony he had again put the lid back on his memory of the gruesome events that had taken place there.

So at first he was pretty angry at me, there on the other end of the line. Later he said what he thought at the time:

"Why would anyone even dream of confronting me with this? It was as if a total stranger had stormed into my house to ask, 'Would you want to talk about Margraten?'" My call had been quite a shock for him. He was totally unprepared for my telephone call.

Jeff had banned Margraten from his mind. He had never talked about it, not to his family, not to friends, not even to his wife Janice, with whom he had been married over forty years. He had told Janice occasionally that he had been to the Netherlands. But the war cemetery: that he never spoke about. It was too painful. The memory of those days took his breath away again. Long ago he had decided to forget all that had anything to do with that period, to forget that he had ever been there.

I realized too late how inconsiderate it had been to confront him out of the blue with that awful period in his life. I still feel ashamed about it even if he forgave me.

I told Jeff that I had gotten his phone number via Sherry Barbour, a neighbor of William Solms, and that I was the project leader of a small team of the local organization in Margraten that was working on an oral history project. And also that we had almost given up hope of being able to get in touch with one of the African American gravediggers of back then. We had found not a single one, despite extensive archive and internet research.

I also told him how important I considered it to be able to interview at least one of the gravediggers of back then. And that the African Americans were regularly mentioned in the interviews with eyewitnesses of the construction of the cemetery. How they spoke with indignation about the way these men were treated. Jeff's anger about being reminded about this awful period in his life slowly subsided. His original skepticism about collaborating with the oral history project ebbed away. He even gradually saw it as his duty towards the nearly twenty thousand people who were buried in Margraten from November 1944 onward. The least he could do was to tell their story of back then. From the perspective of an African American.

Sponsorship funds were immediately applied for so that the film makers could go to the US once again, to interview Jefferson Wiggins at his home in Connecticut.

In September 2009 Jeff Wiggins, Bill Solms, and Sherry Barbour attended the sixty-fifth anniversary of the liberation of Limburg, held in Margraten and Maastricht.* Many journalists sought to interview Wiggins, and on September 10 he was interviewed on Dutch national television. Hardly anything was known at the time about Black American liberators, not in history books, and hardly anything in archives on the war. The only sources were stories that had been kept alive through oral tradition, local papers, and personal journals and diaries.

---

* Wiggins held an impressive speech on September 11, 2009 in the fully packed library of Centre Céramique in Maastricht. Until 2009 hardly anything had been written in the Netherlands about segregation in the US Army, either in books or in archives, except for an article by Cees van Kouwen about African American soldiers who were stationed in and around Nijmegen during Operation Market Garden.

Jeff at Centre Ceramique in Maastricht. Seated: Captain Solms. Standing Janice Wiggins, Malcolm Wiggins, Felicia Wiggins, and Bill Solms Jr. (Photo: Jody Gemmel)

SILENCED AND FORGOTTEN

Jeff: "The fact that the filmmakers' first attempt to find information about the Black Americans of the 960th QMSC failed doesn't surprise me. The main reason for the lack of information about my unit was a major fire on July 12, 1973. That day the buildings of the National Personal Records Center in St. Louis, Missouri went up in flames, causing millions of files to be destroyed, including those of Black veterans. After the fire hardly any records of my unit could be found. Before that fire you could simply walk in and search the archives. All information that you wanted, you could get."

That day the files of about eighty percent of all American soldiers who left military service between November 1, 1912 and January 1, 1960 were lost. That was the main reason for the lack of information. But there were other reasons, too. Data about African Americans were also scarce because their tales after return to the US were seldom put in writing, neither in their own communities nor in national papers. The veteran organizations were predominantly white. Post-war America remained segregated, and, as a result, veteran organizations were mostly taboo for African Americans.

At home there was hardly any audience for their stories. The gap between life in their poor living surroundings and the war in far-away Europe was too wide to bridge for the folks that they came back to. The fact that most African Americans who served during the war carried no guns and did not participate in actual combat is another reason why they were left out of the US history books. For decades their contribution to the European liberation effort remained hidden. In the Netherlands as well.

LATE DECORATIONS

Not a single one of the more than one million African Americans who served during World War II received the Medal of Honor, the highest American military award, during or shortly after the war. This situation only changed in the 1990s, after a study by Shaw University in North Carolina, commissioned by the US Army, revealed that racism had played a role in the awarding of war decorations. This led to the recommendation to nominate various African American soldiers retrospectively for the highest award. As a result, six Distinguished Service Crosses and one Silver Star that African Americans had received were replaced by the Medal of Honor.

This took place on January 13, 1997, more than fifty years after the end of World War II. On that day President Bill Clinton issued the Medal of Honor to seven Black veterans. The only one of these still alive then was Vernon Baker. The others, including Willy F. James Jr., who is buried in Margraten, received the medal posthumously. Many more African Americans received individual decorations in later years. Also, various units were honored retrospectively for their special merits, including the 960th QMSC of Jeff Wiggins.

PASSING ON HISTORY

After my first telephone conversation with Jefferson Wiggins in 2009, several others followed, especially after Jeff had agreed to be interviewed at his home for the Fields of Margraten oral history project.

Jeff: "The more I thought about it, the more I realized – and I still do – that each of us has a place in history. And we need to tell the generations after us what that history has done with us. Film makers Albert Elings and Eugenie Jansen, who were involved in the project, were very professional and dedicated interviewers. At first I thought that it would be one of those standard television interviews that I had encountered before. A journalist would come, ask a few questions, then be off. But the questions that Albert and Eugenie asked were so to-the-point, so investigative, that I suddenly remembered things that I had practically forgotten. For example, they asked, 'What was the weather like in those days? Did you have any contact with the locals? Was your contact with them different from that with fellow Americans there?' I remember that I spoke with Albert about the Dutch children that I met when working there. Something that I had never thought about anymore in all those years."

Jeff Wiggins and Mieke Kirkels before the start of the lecture that he gave at Centre Céramique in Maastricht on September 10, 2009.

CHAPTER 11 – Margraten 2009

In September 2009, Jeff and his wife Janice were invited by the municipality of Margraten for the presentation of the results of the oral history project. They were present at the first showing of the documentary *Akkers van Margraten* (Fields of Margraten) and the presentation of the book *Van boerenakker tot soldatenkerkhof* (From Farmland to Soldiers Cemetery).

Before their arrival, Janice Wiggins told me that her husband still gave lectures in the US about how he grew up in a racially segregated society, both during and after World War II. So I asked him if he would be willing to speak also to a Dutch audience.

The interview by the film makers and the telephone conversations I had with him had convinced Jeff that it was important for him to go back to Margraten. He realized that he was the only person who could tell about the history of the cemetery from the perspective of the 260

African Americans of his unit who had dug so many graves in late 1944 and early 1945. For weeks he locked himself up in his home to consider what he would say in Maastricht.

Before he finally flew to the Netherlands to return to Margraten, Jeff at times enormously regretted his decision to come. As the day of departure approached, his memories of what happened between 1942 and 1945 came back to him. Still, he came.

Jeff: "When we arrived at Amsterdam Schiphol Airport, I knew that it would be a long drive to get to Limburg. The closer I got to Limburg and to Margraten, the more it felt as if history was catching up with me. I said to myself, 'What am I doing here for God's sake?' It was the same question that I had asked myself when I arrived in Margraten in September 1944 for the many weeks of work, without a break, at the cemetery. My wife Janice knew by now what that had involved. I had told her as much as I thought she could handle. That was also more bearable for myself because, thinking back on those days, I couldn't believe that a nineteen-year-old youngster had gotten involved in this. Not just me but my entire unit, in total 260 young Black men aged twenty-two on average.

During my lecture in the library hall of Centre Céramique in Maastricht, I wondered, when I saw the packed room: 'Would the girl from Margraten that I had spoken with at the cemetery gate back then be here in this room?' Then a child, now an elderly woman in the audience?"

MARCH 2010, CONNECTICUT

During his stay in the Netherlands in 2009, Jeff noticed, from the questions that people asked, how little people in Limburg knew about racial segregation in the American army back then.

We applauded the Americans, then and now, for the freedom that they brought Europeans, but that freedom fully contrasted with the racism that was common practice in parts of the US then. Most white Americans knew that, which must have gnawed at the conscience of many.

That is why Jeff hoped that this book would be published and reach many. His intent was to share the tale of the segregation back then with Dutch readers, based on his time in the American army. In March 2010 I visited Jeff and Janice in Connecticut. I interviewed him during a period of two weeks, during filmed sessions that lasted no longer than one hour, since Jeff suffered from the lung disease COPD.

Jeff: "If anyone had told me back then in Alabama that I would one day sit here in this room, talking with a white Dutch woman, looking at a white camerawoman, with my white wife listening to it all, I would have said: you are absolutely crazy. But here we are today, while a Black man is president of the United States, and with many congressmen and congresswomen who are Black. We no longer need to discuss how things ought to be, instead how they are today. For me, a turnabout came somewhere during the war. On the troopship, at the cemetery in Margraten, on the way back home ... somewhere thereabouts it happened."

THE MIND IS THE STANDARD

>Were I so tall to reach the pole,
>Or grasp to the ocean with my span,
>I must be measured by my soul;
>The mind's the standard of the man.
>Isaac Watts, 1674–1748

Jeff: "On the day on which Barack Obama stepped onto the podium to be sworn in as president of the United States, millions of people who ever doubted the saying 'the mind is the standard' discovered how true those words are. President Obama was elected not because of the color of his skin, but because of the state of his mind. Those words should be embedded in the heads of teachers, of legislators, of everyone. The color of your skin is irrelevant. I am especially interested in the thoughts that someone has, in what lives in a person's heart, because that tells me who you are. And I think this applies for millions of others. No one can reverse the changes for the better that have taken place. There are ever fewer people who would want that. The longer I live, the more I notice that. This line from a poem that Dr. King often quoted expresses perfectly that change in mentality."

>The Negro's Complaint (a fragment)
>Fleecy locks and black complexion
>Cannot forfeit nature's claim.
>Skins may differ, but affection

Dwells in white and black the same.
William Cowper, 1731–1800*

CROSSES IN THE WIND

After the interviews with Jeff, I stayed at the Wiggins house for several more days. During a conversation with Jeff and Janice, I mentioned *Crosses in the Wind*, a book written by Joseph James Shomon and originally published in 1947. In this book, Shomon described his experiences during World War II, including a short section about his supervisory role during the construction of the American cemetery in Margraten.

It had never occurred to me that Jeff was not at all familiar with that book, contrary to many other veterans. The reason possibly was that Jeff did not belong to any white veterans' organization. In addition, he had had to struggle to earn a decent living. His prime interest was not at all in his years in the army. Jo Purnot, who died in 2022, a colleague of mine in the *Akkers van Margraten* project, sent Jeff a copy of the book right away.

A few days after my return to the Netherlands, Jeff called me. He had already finished reading Shomon's book and wanted to let me know what he thought of it. He was not amused about the stereotyping, such as in the following quote: "The boys were eating the whole day. Besides the regular food they ate turnips right from the field,

---

* *The Negro's Complaint.* Lines from the poem of that title, written in 1788 by the English poet William Cowper.

apples, pears, even raw potatoes and cabbage. No matter what kind of food it was, so long as there was enough of it. They loved marching to their work in the early morning, with a proud and swift step through the village, [...] and seemed anxious to get started."*

That is how Shomon described the African American grave diggers, and it hurt Jeff deeply. He didn't know what to say. His impression had been that he and the other men were taken seriously at the time by Shomon and other military supervisors, and treated with respect. But what he had read contrasted altogether with that impression. Here, he and his companions were portrayed as dumb workers who only thought of food. Jeff sighed audibly through the phone, and for a while he remained silent. Then he said, "That's how it was in those days." After a few moments he continued: "And that is how it sometimes still is today."

---

* *The Negro's Complaint.* https://allpoetry.com/NYPL

CHAPTER 12 –
People Should Know!

I felt quite honored to be invited by Jeff in 2009 "to do a project with me." Janice smiled when he asked me. She mentioned that he regularly got people to help him with new projects that he came up with but that he could no longer do by himself because of his advanced age and poor health. I felt that no one could ignore such a request, and that applied for me too. I have always referred to the work on this book, including this expanded and revised and translated second edition, as "project Jeff." To some that may not sound very respectful, but Jeff had to laugh every time when I talked with him about "project Jeff." He had a great sense of humor and enjoyed the term.

My wish to pass Jeff's story on to future generations is being fulfilled. That was his intent when he asked me to write this story. He said, "People should know." And today more and more people know that Black Americans were involved in Europe, including in the Netherlands, during

World War II. Soldiers whom I call Black Liberators.

I can only be grateful to Jeff Wiggins, for he has taught me much. Not only through his wise words, reflections, and humor, but also because he introduced me to a piece of history that was altogether new to me.

Time and again I tried to envision, when reading the books and accounts that I used during the writing process, what it must have felt like for African Americans in those days. I tried to imagine how I would have dealt with those circumstances, and where my anger about the humiliations would have left me.

But that is impossible. That is another thing Jeff taught me.

During the years that I worked on Project Jeff, and it is still the case now, I spoke with many people about what he told me and about the historical facts that my research uncovered. Regularly I met people who were totally surprised about the large number of African American soldiers that served in Europe during World War II, who were utterly amazed about the segregation in the American army and about the return of these African Americans after the war to a second-rate existence back home.

I was also amazed that nothing about any of this is to be found in Dutch history books, not even at the Dutch Institute for War Documentation (NIOD).

Fortunately, that situation has changed.

The research that my colleague Sebastiaan Vonk conducted has revealed that at least fifteen thousand African American soldiers were stationed in the Netherlands.

Jeff and Mieke in 2009 in between interviews by Dutch journalists (Photo: Jody Gemmel)

With the support of the Dutch embassy in Washington, DC, Maarten Vleeming searched American archives for descendants of the 172 African Americans buried in Margraten.

This research is still going on.

CHAPTER 13 – A Follow-up Oral History Project

After the liberation from Nazi Germany, roughly ten thousand so-called liberation babies were born in the Netherlands, some seventy of whom were dark-skinned. Approximately thirty of these – they are long since adults – contacted me after the publicity about Jefferson Wiggins' visit. Prior to that, they told me, there was no one that they could tell their story to (or they chose not to). The first of these was Huub Schepers (1945–2016).

In 2015 I decided to start with the oral history project *Children of Black Liberators*. That led to a book of the same title, subtitled *A Suppressed History*, published by Vantilt in 2017. In 2020 an expanded English-language version of this book, which I wrote with Chris Dickon as co-author, was published by McFarland in the US.

CHAPTER 14 – People Should Know, the Sequel

The more I discovered about racism in the American armed forces – and about its demise in more recent years – the more important I considered it to be that further research should be conducted into this subject. This has meanwhile been done by the historian Sebastiaan Vonk. Although I belong to the baby-boom generation, I am not so much interested in World War II as in the stories that people tell.

Partly due to World War II and the civil rights movement that had its roots in that war, life has become somewhat better for African Americans. But racism has not disappeared, in spite of better legislation, and in spite of an African American becoming president of the United States in 2008.

The American cemetery in Margraten is a multicultural cemetery of soldiers of a segregated army. The death certificates of the soldiers display a race code. For the white soldiers who died that is race code 1, for the African Americans it is race code 2. The soldiers are buried at random. I did not talk about this with Jeff, because I was not aware of it at the time. But undoubtedly he would have said, "In death, color doesn't matter."

Several years after the publication of the first edition of this book, the Black Lives Matter movement arose. It was sparked off by the death of Michael Brown, a Black teenager, shot and killed by a white police officer, even though the boy was unarmed. The day after the shooting riots broke out in Ferguson, a suburb of St. Louis, Missouri, where this had happened. More than five hundred people, from various cities in the United States participated in the protests. On July 10, 2016 a first Black Lives Matter protest took place in Amsterdam, in reaction to ongoing police violence in the United States against Black Americans. In response to the death of George Floyd in Minneapolis on May 25, 2020, protests against anti-Black police violence and institutional racism erupted in the US and Europe.

I believe that the Black Lives Matter movement in the Netherlands has contributed to a younger generation now telling the long-forgotten story of the Black liberators. Various projects have meanwhile been carried out or are in process:

- 2017: *Krassen op de huid* (Scarred Skin, at Theater Na de Dam, by Naomi van der Linden and Esther Scheldwacht)
- 2019: "Unique Encounters in Liberated Limburg." Master's thesis by Jules Dresen

- *Black Limburgers* (film by Hans Heijnen)
- *Franklin* (a graphic novel by Brian Elstak and Marga Altena)
- An exhibition at Theater aan het Vrijthof in Maastricht
- *Franklin*, exhibition in Freedom Museum in Groesbeek
- 2021: *Broken Winged Bird* (by Theater Group Maastricht Online)
- 2022: *Children of Black Liberators – Half an American* (documentary by Eric van den Berg and Bram Endedijk broadcast on Dutch National t.v. on May 5 2022. See https://www.2doc.nl/documentaires/2022/05/kinderen-van-zwarte-bevrijders.html
- *Junction*, a theater play by Jasmine van Putten, based on her book
- *The 172 African Americans of Margraten* (documentary and/or book in process of development)
- *The African Americans buried in Margraten* (theater monologues by Black Women's Playwrights Group in Indianapolis, Indiana)[*]

---

[*] Just before the original version of this book went to the printer, we were informed about a production by this American theater group, starting in November 2022, about the 172 African Americans of Margraten.

BLACK AMERICAN VETERANS – OFFICIAL GUESTS IN THE NETHERLANDS

Groups of African Americans were stationed in various locations in the Netherlands during World War II, especially in the provinces of Limburg, Noord-Brabant, and Gelderland. Research by Sebastiaan Vonk revealed that at least fifteen thousand Black American soldiers were stationed in the country. After World War II a small number of Black liberators were in the Netherlands as official guests, in addition to Jefferson Wiggins. The following four veterans were among them.

HENRY BLACKMON*

Blackmon participated in the 3218th Quartermaster Corps of the 1st Army, which was stationed just south of the Netherlands until December 27, 1944. Early in February 1945 this unit was added to the 9th Army, so that he came to be stationed in the vicinity of Kerkrade for a bit over a month. There he assisted in the supply of fuel and food. He also stayed in Maastricht briefly, until his unit left for Bastogne.

He was a good singer, and on the eve of the Battle of the Bulge he was invited to sing during a concert organized by the local authorities of Bastogne. After the battle he helped with the salvaging of corpses, as he had done in Normandy.

Following his return to the US he earned a Bachelor of

---

* In November 2022, Henry Blackmon's son David got in touch with me to say that notes that his deceased father had left evidenced that he had been stationed in the Netherlands during World War II. The notes also mentioned that he had been in the Ardennes, where bodies had to be removed.

Henry Blackmon, born in Four Oaks, North Carolina in 1923, died in The Hague on May 6, 2004 (Source: Blackmon Collection)

Music diploma at Howard University in Washington, DC, taught at Shaw University in Raleigh, North Carolina, and started a singing career. The racial segregation at the time originally prevented him from breaking through. However, his participation in a talent hunt in New York led to a role in the opera *Porgy and Bess*, including a six-months tour through Mexico and Europe. In that capacity he also visited the Netherlands in 1956, where he settled a year later. A successful musical career followed.

Henry Blackmon's honorable discharge card (Source: Blackmon Collection)

He was invited by the city of The Hague on the occasion of his seventy-fifth birthday in 1999, and was received the insignia of knighthood from Wim Deetman, mayor of the city at the time.

TIMUEL D. BLACK
During World War II, Black belonged to the 308th Quartermaster Corps, serving in the Railhead Company, a support group for the railways in Europe. He was called up for military service in 1943, by means of a letter that stated that he was selected "to serve Uncle Sam." Black wrote back that he had no uncle called Sam.

After his training he went to England. From there, the

Timuel D. Black, born in Birmingham, Alabama in 1918, died in Chicago on October 13, 2012 (Source: *The Chicago Maroon*, August 24, 2016)

308th QMSC left for Utah Beach, where it arrived on the fourth day of the invasion.

Letters that he wrote to his folks back home made clear that he was utterly frustrated about the abject discrimination that he experienced in the US Army. Traveling back to the US, he noticed that the German prisoners of war who sailed on the same ship had more rights than he as an African American soldier. The Germans were allowed to be among the white American soldiers, but he couldn't. This convinced Black that he needed to continue the struggle for equal rights in his own country. Along with Black leaders such as Martin Luther King Jr., he grew to become one of the protagonists of the civil rights movement.

Black worked as a history teacher and oral historian and became professor at the City Colleges of Chicago. In 2005 he was invited to come to the Netherlands by the Overseas Americans Remember Foundation (OAR). He was received by the municipal authorities of Eijsden-Margraten and visited the American cemetery.

MATTHEW SOUTHALL BROWN SR.

In 2016, I interviewed Pastor Brown for the oral history project *Children of Black Liberators*. I had come into contact with him via "The 2,221 Negro Infantry Volunteers" organization.

Brown was born in 1922 in Savannah, Georgia and studied at the American Baptist Seminary in Nashville, Tennessee. In February 1943 he was called up for military service, and a year later he left for Europe. At the end of the war he was one of the 2,221 Negro Infantry Volunteers. Following his return to the US, he completed his studies, later becoming pastor of St. John Baptist Church in his home town.

Pastor Brown was honored for his involvement at the Civil Rights Movement several times. Among others: In 2017 he received the Certificate Silver Life Membership from the NAACP (National Association for the Advancement of Colored People). In 2019 – at the anual Dr. Martin Luther King Jr. gala event – he was honored as the Preachers Pastor, for his continuing efforts on behalf of society, both as veteran and visionary.

In May 2019 Pastor Brown contacted me and told me that he was coming to the Netherlands. He had been altogether unaware of the Dutch liberation anniversary celebrations, which was true, he said, for most Black veterans. At the end of the war, liberation celebrations were "for whites only." Pastor Brown was a guest at St. Gerlach Castle in Valkenburg. He was nominated by the American embassy in The Hague to represent the United States in September 2019 at the ceremonies to mark the seventy-fifth anniversary of the liberation in Terneuzen. On that day, ten years after Jefferson Wiggins came to the Netherlands, there was once again lots of attention for the contribution, consigned to silence for so long, of Black American soldiers to the liberation of the Netherlands.

JAMES WILLIE BALDWIN[*]

Baldwin was assigned to the All-Black 784th Tank Battalion, which helped liberate the Dutch town of Venlo. In 1942 he graduated from Laurinburg Institute, a historic African American preparatory school in North Carolina, where he grew up. He then continued his studies at Fayetteville State College. With the help of the GI Bill, he studied psychology and social work at Howard University, the famous first Black university, located in the nation's capital. At the request of the first Black mayor of the city, Walter

---

[*] See Guus Valk, "Een zwarte soldaat met een meisje betekende gedoe," *NRC*, May 2, 2015, https://www.nrc.nl/nieuws/2015/05/ 02/een-zwarte-soldaat-met-een-meisje-betekende-gedoe-1491845-a978769.

James Willie Baldwin, born in Wagram, North Carolina in 1924, died in Washington, DC on August 1, 2022, pictured at the Dutch embassy in Washington, DC

Washington, he led the city's Office of Human Rights. He retired in 1979, but not before he had earned a PhD in public administration at Nova Southeastern University in Fort Lauderdale, Florida.

The 784th Tank Battalion started in April 1943 as part of the 5th Tank Group, along with the African American 758th and 761st Tank Battalions. Baldwin's unit trained in Camp Claiborne in Louisiana. One of the soldiers of this unit called the place a hellhole. African Americans were seriously discriminated against and poorly treated by white members of the military police and bus drivers. Several of his colleagues were not only treated badly and beaten up but even murdered. Compared to this, Fort Hood, Texas,

James Baldwin in 2015 (Photo: Stephan Voss)

where he received a more thorough training, was paradise.

On Christmas Day 1944, his unit arrived in France and then proceeded on towards Germany. The officers and other members of the 104th Infantry Division, which they joined, welcomed the African American unit and helped hem prepare for the terrible winter conditions. As Black liberators, they were also welcomed by the Dutch people. Some of Baldwin's colleagues were killed and subsequently buried in Margraten. The battalion's motto was "It Will Be Done."

An attempt by the municipality of Venlo to organize an official invitation on the occasion of the seventy-fifth anniversary of the liberation failed. Instead, Baldwin was officially received by the Dutch embassy in his hometown of Washington in February 2020.

BATTALION OF THE FORGOTTEN

by Babs Gons, Poet Laureate of the Netherlands 2023-2025

    We buried your dead
    And honored them with peace
    En route to rest eternal
    Won liberation before our own release

    From war to a country
    Where it was not the army we chose
    But rather a future
    Beyond the poor boroughs

    On the same side in the same war
    Fighting for the same ground
    Eyes locked on the same foe
    Marching to the same sound

    But we were made to dig the graves
    Wash the bodies and pack the trucks
    We did the dirty work
    For our white compatriots

We buried your dead
Who in life would not sit with us
Demoted to a world
At the back of the bus

Neither ceremony nor medals
Honors nor accolades
No praise for our triumphs
No turn in the veterans' parades

We were no story
We were never told
No part in the memorial
No hero's glory to hold

We were promised much
More wages and compensation
Higher ranks and promotions
Huge sums of remuneration

And we, in turn, pledged loyalty
To our motherland with pride
Bore the flag with love
Our unity symbolized

We buried others' dead
From a far-flung war
At the burial grounds in Margraten
Left prayers for nevermore

The battalion of the forgotten
The regiment without ballad or song
We fought with you and gave our lives
But were dishonored all along

No reparations
Have yet come our way
We wait in sorrow still
For what should have been our fate

We the forgotten soldiers
Await our due pay
Tribute to our service
The honor of recognition
On this Remembrance Day
The fourth of May

Published May 4, 2023
Translation: Egan Garr

African American relatives of Babs Gons were stationed in Europe during WWII.

More than 1.2 million African American soldiers fought in World War II; over 16,000 were stationed in the Netherlands. They fought for a freedom they did not have at home, but their stories are absent from the prevailing narrative of the war.

Epilogue

There is one person who has done more than anyone else in the Netherlands to bring the stories of the Black Liberators into the light of day: the Dutch oral historian Mieke Kirkels. She is the author of *From Farmland to Soldiers Cemetery, From Alabama to Margraten*, and *Children of Black Liberators*. I interviewed her to hear how she discovered the suppressed history of the participation of African American soldiers during World War II.

Kirkels decided to interview Dutch farmers in the Margraten area for the National Project "Heritage of World War II: Eyewitness Accounts," which started in 2008, to hear what the farmers thought of their farmland becoming a military cemetery. Kirkels' story is filled with remarkable coincidences, such as this one: "In one of the first interviews an older woman told me: 'I felt so sorry for those poor black guys.' I had no idea what she was talking about: to me, the American liberators were white guys with their shiny boots, helmet, and a big smile. But she was talking about black guys having to bury all those bodies! Many of the farmers I interviewed confirmed it."

The revelation that African American soldiers were stationed in the Netherlands prompted Kirkels to try to incorporate them into her project about the cemetery at Margraten. However, by 2009 she had found so little information that she almost decided to continue without their stories. Then, out of the blue, she got an email from the United States. "It sounds like a coincidence, but to me it felt like fate: an American woman wrote to say she was so glad the website about the cemetery at Margraten was in English, since her neighbor had been a US Army captain in World War II."

This neighbor, Captain Solms, turned out to have been in charge of a unit of African American soldiers who dug graves at Margraten. But he was white. Was he by any chance still in touch with any of those African American soldiers? The veterans' organizations were whites-only back then. But Solms had met one of them two years before, and still had his phone number! His name was Dr. Jefferson Wiggins from Connecticut, born in Alabama. Kirkels had interviewed both Dr. Wiggins and Captain Solms, and in September 2009 they came to Margraten to celebrate the sixty-fifth anniversary of the liberation of the Dutch province of Limburg.

Dr. Wiggins asked Kirkels to help him write his memoirs (*From Alabama to Margraten*, published in 2014) of his three years in the segregated US Army during World

War II. She was the only person he had met in the Netherlands who knew of the segregation. That ignorance was not limited to the Netherlands. Kirkels: "American journalists, assigned to travel to Europe with the US Army, were not allowed to write about, or take pictures of the African American soldiers stationed in the Netherlands."

CHILDREN OF BLACK LIBERATORS
Another startling coincidence led to her next project, the book *Children of Black Liberators* (2017). "People could order the book *From Alabama to Margraten* and pick it up themselves. Suddenly there is this man of color standing in front of me. He took my hand and said: 'I am so happy with your book, I have been searching for years in archives for black soldiers stationed here, because my father was one.' His name was Huub Schepers. Eventually, about twenty-five children of African American soldiers reached out and twelve of them were willing to be interviewed. Through this project these 'children of black liberators' became like the family that some of them never had."

Kirkels also interviewed Pastor Matthew Southall Brown Sr., a Black veteran, by phone in 2016. Three years later in May 2019, he emailed her that he wanted to visit the cemetery at Margraten. The American embassy then invited him to represent the US as a guest of honor at the official start of *75 years Freedom* in the Netherlands. Pastor Brown was one of seven veterans present at the commemoration – and the first guest to shake the king's hand. "For me, it has now come full circle."

RACE CODE 2

Kirkels discovered that many African American soldiers are buried at Margraten. Her colleague, researcher Sebastiaan Vonk, made a final list of 172 African Americans who have a grave there. He was able to identify them on the basis of the race code on the burial certificates: *race code 2* were African Americans. With the help of the Dutch Embassy, Vonk started a project in the United States to find and interview relatives of those 172 soldiers, with the aim of telling the story of a group of soldiers who have been forgotten until now. Kirkels: "There are a couple of websites about American cemeteries, but they are just about white American soldiers. We want to give the African American soldiers of Margraten a face and tell their stories."

Jonathan Pieterse, John Adams Institute
Amsterdam, April 2020

For more stories about African American soldiers in the Netherlands and Mieke Kirkels' research, visit https://blackliberators.nl.

Acknowledgements

The first edition of this book could obviously not have been written without the support of Janice Wiggins, the woman with whom Jeff was married for forty-five years. I continue to be especially grateful for her support. After Jeff's death in January 2013 she had to reshape her life. Still, she quickly let me know that she was prepared to again pick up the thread of "Project Jeff." The conversations that we had were very special, emotional at times. Janice and I are still good friends. In May 2023 she was back in Margraten, on the occasion of the opening of Wiggins Park in front of the entrance to the townhall.

Sherryl Hauck, a neighbor of the Wiggins couple, made videos of the long interviews that I had with Jeff in 2020. Without her help I could not have made transcriptions of these. Jeff himself edited the first two chapters of the English-language version of the book. He was not only a good speaker but also a fine writer. He corrected my texts, and in one of the many telephone conversations that we had, I said to him, "This is such beautiful English! Nobody will believe that I wrote this." Jeff answered, "Don't tell."

From that first English draft I prepared the Dutch translation and added historical information. That also meant sketching a picture of the army that Jeff served in and of how the lives of African Americans changed during and as a result of World War II.

During my research I received much support from Frans Roebroeks, both in connection with my research of the archives of the Historisch Centrum Limburg and with the verification of historical facts in the text. Jo Purnot (who died in 2022) helped me greatly with his considerable factual knowledge, the selection of pictures, and his calm assurances when I ran into frustrating matters.

I wish to thank Willemien Lenders, Pauline Broekema, José Mostert, Peter Schrijvers, and (posthumously) Jo Purnot for their comments and encouraging response to the first Dutch draft. And I thank proofreaders Frans Roebroeks and Jettie de Wal for their thoroughness in reading the manuscript and their recommendations for improvement.

Thanks to Joyce Overdijk-Francis, Barbara Oomen, Jacques Vriens, and Ad van Liempt, the very first reviewers of the book.

Anna Wolters undertook the final editing, despite her full diary. The loving, meticulous, and experienced way in which she works made me feel very comfortable.

I am grateful to Wytze Patijn for his encouragement

and support by agreeing to publish the first edition of this book on an in-house basis in 2009.

In addition, I wish to thank the public historian Sebastiaan Vonk, MA, my successor as project manager for www.blackliberators.nl, as he helped me during some ten years in researching data and military information. I am grateful to Art Buro Limburg for the tremendously accurate, pleasant, and supporting ways in which it handled the financial aspects for me.

I was unexpectedly helped at the time by Chris Dickon, an American historian and documentary maker, who contacted me after the publication of *From Farmland to Soldiers Cemetery*. I met him when he visited Margraten on Memorial Day 2014 together with his wife Mary. He researched the copyright situation regarding the historical photos in American archives.

Ms. Alice Mills from Caen in Normandy stimulated me when I was writing the first edition regarding the contribution of African Americans who were involved in the liberation effort. The same applies for Linda Hervieux, a journalist in France and New York.

For the realization of this second edition, which has been expanded with information from follow-up research, I wish to thank the Dutch embassy in Washington, Sebastiaan Vonk, Maarten Vleeming, and Jasmijn Janssen.

I also thank Karel David van der Gun, a very accurate proofreader, who spontaneously offered to help and not only made the necessary corrections but also restructured the text where appropriate.

The opening of Wiggins Park by Janice Wiggins and the American Ambassador Shefali Razdan Duggal, in 2023 (Photo: J.P. Geussens)

Lastly, my thanks go to publisher Leon van Dorp and graphic designer Els Gulpen – both from Heerlen in Southern Limburg –, for publishing the Dutch edition of this book in 2014.

For the realization of the English edition, I thank Ilse Josepha Lazaroms, my editor at Amsterdam University Press. My gratitude also goes to Babs Gons, for giving me permission to use her poem "Batallion of the Forgotten," in an English translation by Egan Garr. I also thank the following institutions for their support of this work: the Netherlands embassy to the United States in Washington, DC; the Netherlands America Foundation; the municipality of Eijsden- Margraten; the Kanunnik Salden Foundation; and the John Adams Institute. Finally, I would like to thank Louis Wong for giving me the reassurance and the space to write.

Literature

"A. Philip Randolph." *History*, October 27, 2009. https://www.history.com/topics/black-history/a-philip-randolph.

Angelou, Maya. *I Know Why the Caged Bird Sings*. New York: Bantam Books, 1988.

Bamat, Joseph. "The Neglected Story of African Americans on D-Day," *France 24*, June 4, 2014. https://www.france24.com/en/20140604-d-day-african-american-battalion-320th-france-scholar-mills-dabney-normandy.

Cowper, William, "The Negro's Complaint." *All Poetry*. https://allpoetry.com/The-Negro's-Complaint.

Dickon, Chris. *The Foreign Burial of American War Dead: A History*. Jefferson, NC and London: McFarland, 2011.

Douglass, Frederick. *Narrative of the Life of Frederick Douglass*. Mineola, NY: Dover Publications, 1995.

Du Bois, W. E. B.. *The Souls of Black Folk: Essays and Sketches*. Mineola, NY: Dover Publications, 1994 (first published 1903).

Gouverne, John. *US Army in Zuid Limburg 1944–1945*. Revised edition.

Maarheeze: self-published, 2011.

Hervieux, Linda. "D-Day." *New York Daily News*, June 5, 2009.

Hervieux, Linda. *Forgotten: The Untold Story of D-Day's Black Heroes, at Home and at War*. New York and London: HarperCollins, 2015.

Kirkels, Mieke, Jo Purnot, and Frans Roebroeks. *Van boerenakker tot soldatenkerkhof. Ooggetuigenverhalen over de aanleg van de Amerikaanse begraafplaats in Margraten*. Margraten: Stichting Akkers van Margraten, 2009.

Kirkels, Mieke, Jo Purnot, and Frans Roebroeks. *From Farmland to Soldiers Cemetery: Eyewitness Accounts of the Construction of the American Cemetery in Margraten*. Margraten: Stichting Akkers van Margraten, 2009.

"Korean War," *History*, May 11, 2022, https://www.history.com/topics/asian-history/korean-war.

Limburg-Margraten 1940–1945. Achtergronden bij tentoonstelling 60 jaar bevrijding van Margraten (September 2004). SHOM/Gemeente Margraten.

Maceda, Jim. "Small Norman Village Honors Fallen Heroes," *NBC*, June 5, 2004, https://www.nbcnews.com/id/wbna5138079.

Mills, Martine-Alice. *Soldats américains noirs, Normandie 1944/Black GIs, Normandy 1944* (Chassignol: Cahiers du Temps, 2014).

Schrijvers, Peter. *The Crash of Ruin: American Combat Soldiers in Europe during World War II*. Houndmills: Macmillan Press, 1998.

Schrijvers, Peter. *Liberators: The Allies and Belgian Society, 1944–1945*. Cambridge: Cambridge University Press, 2009.

Schrijvers, Peter. *De Margraten boys. Hoe een dorp weigerde de Amerikaanse bevrijders te vergeten*. Antwerp: Manteau, 2012.

Schrijvers, Peter. *De schaduw van de bevrijding, België 1944–1945*. 3rd ed. Antwerp: Manteau, 2014.

Shomon, Joseph James. *Crosses in the Wind: Graves Registration Service in the Second World War.* New York: Stratford House, 1947 (available at Stichting Adoptiegraven Margraten)

Shomon, Joseph James. *Kruizen in de wind. De ongeschreven sage van de mannen in de Amerikaanse Gravendienst in de Tweede Wereldoorlog.* 3rd ed. Translated by M. M. C. Kessels (available at Stichting Adoptiegraven Margraten)

Sledge, Michael. *Soldier Dead: How We Recover, Identify, Bury and Honor Our Military Fallen.* New York: Columbia University Press, 2007.

Wilson, Woodrow. "My Fellow Countrymen ..." July 26, 1918. Library of Congress Printed Ephemera Collection; portfolio 241, folder 18.

Takaki, Ronald. *A Different Mirror: A History of Multicultural America.* Boston: Back Bay Books, 1993.

Valk, Guus. "Een zwarte soldaat met een meisje betekende gedoe." *NRC*, May 2, 2015. https://www.nrc.nl/nieuws/2015/05/02/een-zwarte-soldaat-met-een-meisje-betekende-gedoe-1491845-a978769.

Vonk, Sebastiaan, contributions on https://blackliberators.nl/.

"Who Are the Tuskegee Airmen of World War II," Tuskegee Airmen National Historical Museum, https://tuskegeemuseum.org/history/#:~:text=Who%20are%20the%20Tuskegee%20Airmen,skill%2C%20courage%2C%20and%20patriotism.

Wiggins, Jefferson. *Another Generation Almost Forgotten.* N.p.: XLibris, 2003.

Websites consulted

www.akkersvanmargraten.nl

www.blackliberators.nl

For Product Safety Concerns and Information please contact our EU representative GPSR@taylorandfrancis.com
Taylor & Francis Verlag GmbH, Kaufingerstraße 24, 80331 München, Germany

www.ingramcontent.com/pod-product-compliance
Lightning Source LLC
Chambersburg PA
CBHW051101230426
43667CB00013B/2396